WALT DISNEY

WALT DISNEY

A Biography

Louise Krasniewicz

GREENWOOD BIOGRAPHIES

 GREENWOOD

AN IMPRINT OF ABC-CLIO, LLC
Santa Barbara, California • Denver, Colorado • Oxford, England

Library of Congress Cataloging-in-Publication Data

Krasniewicz, Louise, 1952-
    Walt Disney : a biography / Louise Krasniewicz.
        p. cm. — (Greenwood biographies)
    Includes bibliographical references and index.
    ISBN 978-0-313-35830-2 (hard copy : alk. paper) —
    ISBN 978-0-313-35831-9 (ebook)
  1. Disney, Walt, 1901–1966.   2. Animators—United States—Biography.
  I. Disney, Walt, 1901–1966.   II. Title.
    NC1766.U52D5452   2010
    791.43092—dc22
    [B]   2010015896

ISBN: 978-0-313-35830-2
EISBN: 978-0-313-35831-9

14 13 12 11 10   1 2 3 4 5

This book is also available on the World Wide Web as an eBook.
Visit www.abc-clio.com for details.

Greenwood
An Imprint of ABC-CLIO, LLC

ABC-CLIO, LLC
130 Cremona Drive, P.O. Box 1911
Santa Barbara, California 93116-1911

This book is printed on acid-free paper ∞

Manufactured in the United States of America

CONTENTS

SERIES FOREWORD

In response to high school and public library needs, Greenwood developed this distinguished series of full-length biographies specifically for student use. Prepared by field experts and professionals, these engaging biographies are tailored for high school students who need challenging yet accessible biographies. Ideal for secondary school assignments, the length, format, and subject areas are designed to meet educators' requirements and students' interests.

Greenwood offers an extensive selection of biographies spanning all curriculum related subject areas including social studies, the sciences, literature and the arts, history and politics, as well as popular culture, covering public figures and famous personalities from all time periods and backgrounds, both historic and contemporary, who have made an impact on American and/or world culture. Greenwood biographies were chosen based on comprehensive feedback from librarians and educators. Consideration was given to both curriculum relevance and inherent interest. The result is an intriguing mix of the well known and the unexpected, the saints and sinners from long-ago history and contemporary pop culture. Readers will find a wide array of subject choices from fascinating crime figures like Al Capone to inspiring

pioneers like Margaret Mead, from the greatest minds of our time like
Stephen Hawking to the most amazing success stories of our day like
J. K. Rowling.

　　While the emphasis is on fact, not glorification, the books are meant
to be fun to read. Each volume provides in-depth information about
the subject's life from birth through childhood, the teen years, and
adulthood. A thorough account relates family background and education, traces personal and professional influences, and explores struggles,
accomplishments, and contributions. A timeline highlights the most
significant life events against a historical perspective. Bibliographies
supplement the reference value of each volume.

PREFACE

Everybody knows Walt Disney. Walt, as he always preferred to be called, was the father of Mickey Mouse, the designer of Disneyland, and the man who made millions of people believe that, indeed, dreams can come true. But the real Walt Disney was a man of many facets and from his birth at the beginning of the 20th century to his death in 1966, he influenced more aspects of everyday American life than any other individual.

Walter Elias Disney was born in Chicago on December 5, 1901, the fourth son of Elias and Flora Disney, hardworking Midwesterners. In 1906, the Disneys left Chicago and settled in Marceline, Missouri. Years later, after he became famous, Walt would fondly remember his four years in Marceline and use the town as his model for the ideal, nostalgic America. The family moved to Kansas City after hard times on the farm. Walt never did very well in school and was often being caught doodling and daydreaming.

Walt's interest in art was encouraged by some family members and after a move back to Chicago he took a few art classes. But World War I was raging and Walt, faking the birth date on his birth certificate because at 16 he was too young to join up, eventually ended up with the

Red Cross in Europe. There he expanded his artwork, designing Red Cross posters and editorial cartoons. Back in Kansas City after the war, Walt landed a job doing commercial art. He experimented with animations, selling a few but eventually going bankrupt.

Taking his art supplies and a dream of making it in Hollywood, Walt headed west in 1923 and joined his brother Roy in California. Together they opened the first Disney studio and began producing innovative short movies about the adventures of a little girl that combined live action and animation. Contracts to produce this *Alice* series resulted in 54 *Alice* films but also a chance to animate a new character: Oswald the Lucky Rabbit. By this time the studio had expanded to include several talented animators and these men were eventually secretly lured away by Walt's shifty New York agent.

Walt also found out that he did not own the rights to Oswald. On his way back to California on a cross-country train after hearing this, Walt began developing a new character for his animations: Mortimer Mouse! Walt's wife Lilly suggested a more appropriate name, Mickey, and an icon was born. Loyal Disney animator Ub Iwerks helped Walt design and animate the new character. Mickey was supposed to begin appearing in a series of cartoons, but only the first one was released before an innovation shook the film world. Almost all movies, including cartoons, to this point had been silent, but the introduction of sound in 1927 inspired Walt.

In 1928, Walt released *Steamboat Willie*, the first sound cartoon. It starred Mickey Mouse who became a cultural sensation. Mickey was one of the first animated characters to appear on a wide range of merchandise, and the Disney studio developed the standards for merchandise tie-ins that all media production companies now emulate. By 1930, millions of kids joined Mickey Mouse Clubs and bought hundreds of different Mickey Mouse items.

The studio continued to produce Mickey cartoons and began a new series called *Silly Symphonies*, which were nonlinear animations inspired by music. They were popular and financially successful. One *Silly Symphony*, *Flowers and Trees*, was released as the first all-color cartoon. In 1932, *Flowers and Trees* won an Academy Award and the same year Walt received a special Oscar for developing Mickey Mouse. Another *Silly Symphony*, *Three Little Pigs*, won an Oscar in 1934 and spawned another cultural phenomenon with merchandise purchases and popular songs, all now licensed by the Disneys.

Despite the economic downturn of the Great Depression, Walt's studio still employed many animators, and they began working on the first feature-length animation, *Snow White and the Seven Dwarfs*. *Snow White* was released in 1937 and was a huge hit, playing in theatres around the world for the next year. It resulted in another special Academy Award for Walt. In 1938 Walt received honorary master's degrees from Yale, Harvard, and University of Southern California, but he also lost his mother Flora in an accident at the California house that he and brother Roy had just bought for their parents.

The money from *Snow White* enabled the studio to move into a new building that was specially designed by Walt for animation work. Animators were now working on several movies that became known as Disney Classics: *Pinocchio, Bambi, Fantasia,* and *Dumbo,* all of which were released in the next several years. World War II had begun in Europe, and this shut off European markets for Disney animations. At the same time, Disney animators and other staff began asking for better working conditions and consistent work rules. By early 1941, talk of a strike developed, and by the summer of 1941 hundreds of staff were on strike.

Walt was upset that the staff he had nurtured and kept employed during the Depression had turned on him and were being disloyal, just like his earlier Oswald staff who left him. Walt put ads in local newspapers calling the union organizers communist agitators. As negotiations continued, Walt agreed to go to South America for the U.S. government to promote cooperation so they would not affiliate with the war's Axis powers. While he was out of the country shooting footage and making friends, Walt's father died and the strike was settled. Walt returned with enough footage to produce several Latin American movies that expanded the Disney market in new directions.

In December 1941, America entered World War II and the Disney studio was immediately occupied by soldiers whose duty was to protect the nearby military industries. By the time they left several months later, Walt had begun production on instructional and propaganda films for the U.S. military and several government agencies. This work was to have a lasting effect on the studio and the culture because Walt encouraged the use of animation for the teaching of mundane tasks and for the spread of pro-government propaganda. Walt developed a series of cartoons encouraging citizens to pay their taxes. For the military he showed soldiers with a minimal education how to prepare their weapons and make battlefield decisions. On his own he developed a film called *Victory through Air Power* that promoted the belief that planes rather than ships were the key to military victory. His animators produced several anti-Hitler cartoons, like Donald Duck's *Der Fuehrer's Face*, which were very popular.

After the war the studio became substantially smaller when government contracts ended. While animating several feature length films continued, Walt testified in Washington, D.C. at one of the many hearings that were investigating communists in Hollywood. Still smarting from the betrayals he saw in his striking animators, Walt was one of the "friendly" witnesses who "named names," citing several of his workers as communists or people who acted like communists. The hearings, beyond Walt's testimony, resulted in a Hollywood blacklist that continued for years, depriving many talented artists of the right to work.

Walt spent time rebuilding the studio but also moved in new directions. He developed his interest in trains and visited the Chicago Railroad Fair in 1948. There and at a nearby historic village, he picked up some ideas for an amusement park, "Mickey Mouse Park," which he wanted to build near his studio to entertain visitors. Walt also visited Alaska and there developed an interest in producing nature films. In 1948, the first *True-Life Adventure*, about seals in Alaska, was released and the next year it won an Academy Award. The *True-Life Adventures* are considered among the earliest nature films that influenced several generations to think about ecology and protecting wildlife.

The end of the war reopened European markets but much of the studio's money was tied up by European government regulations. Walt decided to use that money to create live-action movies that were produced in England. A series of successful movies, starting with *Treasure Island* in 1950, were released. Walt had not forgotten the plans for the Mickey Mouse Park. He developed his own company, WED Enterprises, to begin developing the park, now called Disneyland. Property was purchased in Southern California and funding procured from banks. Walt developed the park with his Imagineering staff, applying his interest in trains and miniatures to the design. The goal was a family-oriented theme park that was fun, clean, and safe for the entire family.

Disneyland opened in July 1955, and the opening was broadcast to 90 million television viewers, many of whom watched the development of the park through Walt's weekly television program, which started in 1954. Disneyland attracted nearly 5 million people in its first year and became the model for all subsequent theme parks. Walt began looking for the location that would make the ideal home for a second park, on the East Coast. Disneyland took much of Walt's attention since it was continually expanding and changing, experimenting with new attractions and technologies.

One of the developing technologies came to be known as Audio-Animatronics, and it provided realistic movement and sound to attraction animal figures, human figures, and objects. Walt saw an opportunity to refine and extend the capabilities of Audio-Animatronics when he contracted with three corporations and one state to build their pavilions at the 1964–65 World's Fair in New York. Four attractions designed for the World's Fair—"it's a small world," "Primeval World," "Great Moments with Mr. Lincoln," and "Progressland"—eventually ended up at Disneyland. Audio-Animatronics influenced the development of attractions, displays, and rides around the world as well as the special effects in motion pictures.

By 1965, 50 million people had visited Disneyland, and Walt and his brother Roy were moving ahead with a new park in Florida, one that included an experimental city and a focus on technologies that could improve the lives of people everywhere. The studio continued to develop live action movies, including *Mary Poppins*, which won several Academy Awards, bringing the studio's total under Walt's leadership to 48. But by 1966, Walt was ill and discovered to have lung cancer. Shortly after his diagnosis, he died and was quietly cremated (not cryogenically frozen as urban legend would have it) in California. His brother Roy renamed the project in Florida Walt Disney World and opened it before his own death, a short time later, in 1971. The Disney name has since been associated with the same type of family-oriented entertainment, a nostalgia for simpler times, and a belief in the inherent goodness of Americans that Walt started so many years earlier.

ACKNOWLEDGMENTS

Thank you:

To all the previous biographers of Walt Disney and his enterprises: Even if I did not always agree with your analyses or conclusions, I now appreciate the enormity of the task and the difficulty of understanding such a complex man. All your work has been appreciated.

To all the animators who have worked in the history of the medium, and their comic book counterparts, for creating imaginative worlds that carry out the fine tradition of mythmaking for our culture. Like Walt, they have shown the true heart of cinema resides in this illusion of life.

To the passionate and devoted bloggers and webmasters of the Disney online universe: many of the sources quoted in this book would not have been easily available just a few years ago. Now, Disney sites provide invaluable information to the Disney researcher and your hard work is indispensable.

To the Barstow family for sharing their wonderful adventures on film, and especially to Robbins Barstow for his gracious communications. Thanks for the wonderful reminder of what Walt was trying to accomplish.

To Ray Bradbury, for always defending Walt in plain English and with the fervor that comes from understanding the genius of the man, a genius he shared with his friend and collaborator.

To my usual coauthor, Michael Blitz, who graciously let me explore Walt on my own and provided moral support just at the right moment. We will continue moving on in magical projects together.

To Richard Leventhal, for being willing to take one more trip to the Magic Kingdom even when it seemed less than enchanting and for willingly riding "it's a small world" one more time.

To my wonderful son, Drew, who has shared my Disneyland enthusiasm since his birth and has agreeably participated in the family ritual of measuring growth by riding a new ride each year. This book is dedicated to you: Believe in the magic and "dream yourself into being."

INTRODUCTION:
MAN, MYTH, AND MOUSE

He gave us Mickey Mouse, Donald Duck, Snow White, and Bambi. His movies, books, comics, merchandise, and television programs have enchanted several generations of children and adults both in America and around the world. He developed the theme park into a dream family destination, providing fun, safe, and affordable adventures for millions of people. He became a major public figure and associated with kings and presidents and movie stars. He changed the way Hollywood made movies with his innovative animations and his mainstream, family-oriented motion pictures. He perfected the model of merchandise tie-ins and entered nearly every American home with his images, stories, or ideals.

But Walt Disney is dead and has been since 1966. The cause of his death is not a mystery: he smoked all his life and succumbed to lung cancer. Despite urban legends that have him preserved in a cryogenic freeze, ready to be thawed out when science deems it possible, he and his body are gone, and his ashes are buried in a cemetery in California. News of the death of Walt Disney stunned his employees who were not generally aware of the seriousness of his illness. News of his death shocked the world because when he died at age 65, he had been involved in so many projects in so many places that it seemed like he was everywhere, and always would be.

And indeed, anywhere you go in America, and at many other places you go in the world, you would swear that Walt Disney was alive and well and still filling the culture with his imaginative creations and manufactured products. The fascination with Walt Disney has been a part of the American way of life for nearly 100 years, and his death did not stop the speculations, disenchantments, wonder, and curiosity about Disney. Walt (for he wanted to be called Walt above all else) stepped into iconic status very early in his life as an animator, and his maintenance of that status long after his physical death (and long after he stopped cartooning) is a definite indication of his significant if controversial contributions to American culture.

But just what are those contributions and why, 40-plus years after his death, does he continue to be a figure of love and admiration but also controversy and even face-reddening, head-shaking, venom-spewing hatred? Biographer Richard Schickel, who created his critical account of Walt soon after he died, wrote as if Walt, for all the imaginative things he did, needed to be taken down a few notches. For Schickel and many other critics, the world was tricked into thinking that Walt simply wanted to fulfill the goal of making everyone happy instead of the corporate goal of making lots of money. Biographer Marc Elliot went further and created a radical image of the same man as a drunken, repressed, and depressed man with questionable personal behavior and radically conservative political leanings. Yet other biographers struggled with admiring the creative man but feeling obligated to deconstruct the corporate or personal human behind the Mickey machine.

Is it just that we never let our larger-than-life icons get too big before we start whittling away at their magical aura, or was Walt Disney such a complex and contradictory man that it was inevitable he would spawn endless incompatible images that circulate to this day: Walt Disney the imaginative but financially shaky businessman; Uncle Walt the genial television host; Mr. Disney the tyrannical boss; Walter Elias Disney the turn-of-the-century small town boy; or Walter E. Disney, "producer of motion-picture cartoons," who gave friendly testimony in a 1947 Congressional hearing that was seeking evidence on communists in Hollywood? Is he Walt the animator and cartoonist, Walt the creator of themed vacation destinations, Walt the World's Fair genius, Walt the friend of the famous and the powerful, Walt the eternal child, Walt the fragile and depressed adult man, the control freak, the husband, the loyal brother and son, an FBI informant, the father of Pinocchio and Dumbo? Is he our own "Jiminy Cricket," both our cultural conscience and our sanitized swear word? Can one man be all these things, and is it just this versatility or uncertainty that creates both his ardent admirers and his passionate critics? Or are we all just Imagineering too much and is Walt Disney and all he stood for dead, never to be unfrozen?

A psychological portrait of Walt Disney would have the faults of every such speculative picture: you can never know what was in a man's head, what his motivations and muses and misgivings really were. Walt commented often on what he was doing, but his account doesn't always match that of his biographers years later. Such a psychological portrait would fail in the attempt to get at the man and not incidentally gives short shrift to the culture that the man both functioned in and helped create. As historian Ray Raphael explains about all out national myths and our sense of history, we tend to act as if "historical actors function as autonomous bundles of free will, devoid of context" and that they are not products of their times and places.[1]

What was it, then, about the 1920s that could inspire a Midwestern boy to create a new form of moving images? What was it that made it possible for Walt Disney to be blind to the changes in American life that led to his devastating animators' strike in the early '40s? Why was it possible for Disney to instantly shift to producing World War II propaganda and then see communists a few years later behind Hollywood cameras, scripts, and studio doors? Was it just shrewdness that led him into nature films in the 1940s or something in the cultural air that directed his imagination that way? Was Disneyland just a plan for a cleaner family park that people could attend in the rigid and bland 1950s, or was it a place that let Walt materialize his own fantastic dreams? Was the New York World's Fair in 1964–65 the birthplace of audio-animatronics and human robotics, or did years of technological miniaturizing make "Great Moments with Mr. Lincoln" possible?

Walt Disney was born in 1901, just as the new millennium was beginning, and during the first half of the 20th century he helped reshape the way America told its history, used its leisure time, spent its money, and thought about itself. He became known around the world as Walt or even Uncle Walt, and through his use of imagination and innovation, he created the world of entertainment and media cross-overs that we experience today. Yet this same man, whose onscreen alter-ego is a mouse with a high voice named Mickey, has been accused of some of the most antisocial crimes: warping the minds of children, dominating the media, informing for the FBI, busting unions in his own businesses, and redefining reality itself for his own political agen-das. Was he the Uncle Walt who cared more than anything for the fantasy worlds he created for everyone, or was he a mean-spirited and vindictive man who cared more than anything about power and how he could wield it?

Sorting out the mythology of Walt Disney—Why did he like trains? Was he bigoted? Did he make the first-ever nature films? Where did he get his animation ideas from? Was he the first man to be cryogeni-cally frozen?—is an adventure that Walt himself would have enjoyed. It travels from the heartland of America into the hearts of children and adults everywhere; it reveals secrets about a country that was struggling with its politics and position in the world; it provides mild scares and predictable shocks but also the trademark Disney nostalgia for simpler and easier times; it looks both to the conservative past and the vision-ary future as it explores a man who had one foot in each and showed us how the two were not incompatible in his America. That there was not just one Walt Disney that can be pinned down and easily defined should not be discouraging. As his nephew Roy E. Disney was fond of saying, "If you get forty people in a room together and ask each one of them to write down who Walt was, you'd get forty different Walts."[2]

But looking at Walt Disney as merely a historic figure who influenced the reading, viewing, leisure, and buying habits of several generations is to miss the essence of "Uncle Walt": he was a part of our lives and all the details of union strikes and hunting communists and bargaining hard in business don't seem to matter to most people's everyday lives. What does matter, and has throughout Uncle Walt's presence in the culture, has been his most amazing and unprecedented reach into so many aspects of our existence. What matters most about Walt Disney is how everyday people have been affected by his work. So while the academics and the historians and the politicians argue about the value of, or damaged cause by, his work, millions of people are still joyfully watching movies he produced, enjoying television shows inspired by his values, and visiting magic kingdoms that carry out his dreams. The real task is not to ferret out the true and unvarnished Walt Disney but to show the fallout and effects of his life, his deeds, and his ideas, even long after his death.

Whether you see a trip to Disneyland, Walt's original theme park, as a mechanism for corporate America to suck dollars out of your pocket through incessant merchandising, or you see it as a chance to share, even for just a short time, the dream world that Walt Disney created, then Disney has affected your life. If you see a Disney movie as a safe bet on a rainy afternoon when all the rest of the world offers violent, sexualized, and explosion-driven cinema, or you instead see the same movie as unbearable, watered-down pabulum for the masses, then Disney has touched your life too. Because whether Disney makes you cringe or cry for joy, whether you smile or scream at the mention of Mickey Mouse and his pals, Walt Disney's creations are part of our cultural experience, and the culture that materializes the Disney touch is here whether we approve or not.

It is this touch that is Walt Disney's most important contribution, and it is a touch not just buried in corporate greed but one that demonstrates a most human trait: the desire, need, and will to connect with others in order to prove our own humanity. Too heady a concept for a subject as mundane as a man who created cartoons and fake Main Streets? Not if we think of the popular culture that Disney both embraced and generated as the shadowland where our mythical stories are played out not only with our passive consent, but with our active participation. Our physical embrace of things and places Disney are not necessarily a cultural weakness but rather cultural signposts, indicators of our willingness to follow the lead that Disney himself relished. There may be more elegant playgrounds than Disneyland, and more artistic drawings than those of Steamboat Willy, but there has yet to be a form of human contact more readily accessible and widely experienced than that imagined and materialized by Walt Disney.

Maybe some people really can't stand anything associated with Disney because Walt did two things that are not supposed to be humanly possible: he materialized dreams and he defied the logic of life by being one of those individuals who affects history as much as he was affected by it. For either of these qualities he could be both suspect and adored; having both of them puts him in a category that few can carry without serious backaches. How one man, starting with a pencil and some dreams, touched the world in a way few men have is the story of Walt Disney. Futurist, businessman, animator, film producer, writer, philanthropist, magician, dreamer, "Imagineer," icon, and symbol: how one man took on all these roles and changed a culture is not only the story of Walt Disney but also the story of America in the 20th century and beyond.

In a review of an earlier biography of Walt Disney, the eminent science fiction writer Ray Bradbury bluntly stated, "I don't, of course, for a moment believe that Uncle Walt can be explained."[3] Bradbury, however, was not suggesting that it wasn't worth exploring Disney's accomplishments. On the contrary, he said that this story of a free spirit who failed over and over again was a great story and that those who fail to see this are simply afraid of what they would have to face if, indeed, we could make dreams come true as Disney always promised, or threatened. Disney's legacy, he explained beautifully, can be summed up by connecting Walt to our cultural dreams: "Our dreams are immortal because in our time, men like Disney have helped us invent proper robot devices to butterflynet-trap Time and Space and Idea so we can walk around them and measure and find them good or bad, mark our shadows on the sill to see, my God, how we have grown."[4]

At the center of the hub that provides access to all the world of the Magic Kingdom at Disneyland in California is a life-size bronze statue of Walt Disney. Called "Partners," it was designed by the legendary Disney sculptor Blaine Gibson as a tribute to Mickey Mouse's 65th birthday and was erected in 1993; a nearly identical statue stands at Walt Disney World in Florida. The Walt shown here is mature and dignified in his conservative suit and calm expression. He is gesturing with his right hand toward Main Street, and his left hand is held by a child-sized Mickey Mouse who comes just about up to his waist. The plaque on the stand reads, "I think most of all what I want Disneyland to be is a happy place ... Where parents and children can have fun, together. Walt Disney." The statue was "rededicated" on December 5, 2001, in celebration of Walt's 100th birthday. A new plaque reads: "as a tribute to the Dreams, Creativity and Vision of WALT DISNEY whose legacy reaches into a new century around the world and here, 'Where the Magic Began.'"

All day, every day, for hours and without end, people who are visiting the park come up to circle where the statue stands and have a picture taken in front of it. Mickey and Walt, in photos saved and displayed around the world, stand behind visitors who speak different languages and wear different clothes, who are better or less well off, who are all ages and all nationalities. Recently at Disneyland, a family with reluctant teenagers stood in front of the statue for the requisite photo. When one of the teens objected and wanted to know why she had to stand just there, someone in her party explained in exasperation, "Because it's Walt Disney, stupid!"

NOTES

1. Raphael, Ray. *Founding Myths: Stories That Hide Our Patriotic Past*. New York: New Press, 2004.

2. Green, Amy Boothe, and Howard E. Green. *Remembering Walt: Favorite Memories of Walt Disney*. New York: Hyperion, 1999, p. xi.

3. Bradbury, Ray. "Walt Disney, the Man Who Invented a Better Mouse." *Los Angeles Times*, November 14, 1976, p. U3.

4. Ibid.

TIMELINE: EVENTS IN THE LIFE OF WALT DISNEY

1801	Arundel Elias Disney, Walt's great-grandfather, is born in Ireland.
1834	Kepple Disney, Walt's grandfather, is born.
1836	Arundel Disney and family emigrate to New York.
1858	Kepple Disney marries Mary Richardson.
1859	Kepple and Mary have a son, Elias, Walt's father.
1888	Elias marries Flora Call and they settle in central Florida.
	Son Herbert is born.
1890	Elias moves his family to Chicago, works as a carpenter at the World's Fair.
	Son Raymond is born.
1893	Son Roy O. Disney is born.
December 5, 1901	Walter Elias Disney born.
1903	Daughter Ruth is born.
1906	The Disney family moves to Marceline, Missouri.
1909	Walt first attends the Park School when he is nearly eight.
1910	The Disney family sells off its belongings and farm.

1911   The Disney family moves to Kansas City.
       Walt attends the Benton Grammar School.
       Walt works his father's paper route.
1914   World War I begins.
1916   Elias decides to move the family back to Chicago.
       Walt stays in Kansas City.
1917   Walt and Ruth graduate from Benton Grammar School.
       Walt takes a summer job working on the railroad.
       Walt enrolls in McKinley High School in Chicago.
       Walt attends art classes at the Art Institute of Chicago.
1918   Walt works at the Chicago post office and nearly misses being injured by a bomb.
       Walt and a friend try to join the Red Cross Ambulance Corp and fake their birth dates to get in.
       Walt contracts the flu and is nursed at home by his mother.
       World War I ends.
       Walt is sent to Europe as a driver for the Red Cross.
1919   Walt returns from his year in Europe with enough money to set up his own business.
       Walt moves to Kansas City and meets Ub Iwerks at the Pesmen-Rubin Art Studio.
       Walt and Ub Iwerks establish their own commercial art business, Iwwerks-Disney.
       Walt leaves to work for the Kansas City Slide Company.
1920   Iwwerks-Disney goes bankrupt.
       Ub goes to work with Walt at the Kansas City Slide Company.
1921   Walt begins producing Newman's Laugh-O-grams.
1922   Walt releases his first animated cartoon, *Little Red Riding Hood*.

Walt establishes Laugh-O-gram Films and gets a contract for six cartoons.

Walt makes *Tommy Tucker's Tooth* for a local dentist.

1923 Walt contacts New York distributor Margaret Winkler about his *Alice* films.

First *Alice* film, *Alice's Wonderland*, starring Virginia Davis, completed.

Laugh-O-grams goes bankrupt.

Walt takes a train to Los Angeles where his brother Roy already lives.

Walt receives contract from Margaret Winkler for a series of *Alice* films.

1924 Lillian Bounds begins to work at the Disney Bros. Studio.

The first *Alice* movie is shown in theatres followed by a new release every few weeks.

Ub Iwerks moves to Los Angeles to work at the studio.

1925 More *Alice* comedies are completed and released.

April Roy marries Edna Francis.

July Walt marries Lillian Bounds.

1926 Walt and Roy finish construction of a new studio.

Margaret Mintz suggests that Walt produce a new cartoon character, a rabbit.

The *Alice* series continues.

1927 Oswald the Lucky Rabbit cartoon series begins.

The last (54th) *Alice* movie is released.

1928 Walt goes to New York to negotiate a new Oswald contract with Charles Mintz.

Mintz hires away several key Disney animators.

Mintz claims the Oswald character.

Walt develops the idea for Mickey Mouse on the train back to Los Angeles.

Ub Iwerks refines Mickey and begins work on Mickey cartoons.

The first silent Mickey Mouse cartoon, *Plane Crazy,* is shown.

Production on the first sound Mickey cartoon, *Steamboat Willie,* begins.

Walt signs an agreement with Pat Powers to represent the studio.

Steamboat Willie debuts in a New York theatre.

1929   Ub Iwerks creates *The Skeleton Dance.*

The *Silly Symphony* series begins.

The Great Depression begins.

1930   The first official Mickey Mouse Clubs begins.

Ub Iwerks leaves the studio to work for Pat Powers.

Roy signs the first contract for Disney merchandise.

The first Mickey Mouse comic strip appears in a newspaper.

Walt and Roy sever their distribution relationship with Pat Powers.

1931   The studio continues to produce Mickey cartoons and *Silly Symphonies*.

Walt reveals decades later that he suffered a nervous breakdown this year.

1932   Roy signs a contract with "Kay" Kamen to negotiate merchandise rights.

The first full color cartoon, *Flowers and Trees,* is released.

Art classes for the studio animators begin.

Walt receives a special Academy Award for the creation of Mickey Mouse.

Flowers and Trees receives an Academy Award.

1933   Mickey Mouse watches are produced.

1934   *Three Little Pigs* receives an Academy Award.

Work begins on the first feature-length animation, *Snow White and the Seven Dwarfs*.

1935   Walt receives the League of Nations award in France.

Lionel produces a Mickey Mouse train car.

Work continues on *Snow White*.

1936 Work continues on *Snow White.*

1937 Work continues on *Snow White.*

Production begins on *Bambi* and *Pinocchio.*

The Old Mill, with the first use of a multiplane camera, is released.

Snow White and the Seven Dwarfs opens successfully in Hollywood.

1938 Leopold Stokowski begins work on *The Sorcerer's Apprentice.*

Disney animators begin to meet to talk about work conditions.

The Old Mill wins an Academy Award.

Walt receives honorary master's degrees from the University of Southern California, Yale, and Harvard.

Walt joins the Society of Independent Motion Picture Producers (SIMPP).

Flora Disney, Roy and Walt's mother, dies in a house accident.

1939 Walt receives a special Academy Award for *Snow White and the Seven Dwarfs.*

Disney artifacts are included in the New York World's Fair time capsule.

An in-house union of cartoonists is created.

The staff begins move into its new studio in Burbank.

World War II begins in Europe; the market for film releases there closes.

1940 *Pinocchio* is released.

Public stock is offered in Walt Disney Productions.

Fantasia is released.

Activity increases in the cartoonist unions including the external Screen Cartoonists Guild.

1941 *Pinocchio* wins Academy Awards for best song and best musical score.

The studio produces four war films for the National Film Board of Canada.

Negotiations between the studio and the cartoonists union fail to produce an agreement.

Animator Art Babbitt is fired for his union work.

Studio staff goes on strike and picket outside the studio.

The Reluctant Dragon is released.

Walt runs an ad in several newspapers calling the strike the result of communist agitation.

Walt goes to South America at the request of the U.S. government.

Walt's father Elias dies while he is on the trip.

The strike is settled and the staff is reduced.

Dumbo is released.

Pearl Harbor is attacked, America enters World War II, the Disney studio is occupied by military forces.

Walt begins producing government films.

1942　Walt finishes many instructional films for the government including *The New Spirit*, a Donald Duck film about paying taxes.

Bambi is released.

Saludos Amigos is released in South America.

1943　*Der Fuehrer's Face* is released and wins an Academy Award.

The Spirit of '43 Donald Duck tax film is released.

More instructional films for the government are finished.

Victory through Air Power is released.

1944　*Snow White and the Seven Dwarfs* is rereleased.

The studio produces several dozen short instructional films for the military.

The Three Caballeros is released in Mexico.

1945　More films for the U.S. Army and other government agencies are produced.

World War II ends.

1946　*Fantasia* and *Dumbo* are rereleased.

Hundreds of staff are laid off at the studio.

Song of the South is released.

1947 Walt and daughter Sharon visit Alaska.
Walt testifies in Washington at the HUAC hearings looking for communists in Hollywood.

1948 *Song of the South* wins two Academy Awards.
Production begins on the *True-Life Adventure* series.
Walt visits the Chicago Railroad Fair and Greenfield Village with animator Ward Kimball.
Walt sketches out a plan for "Mickey Mouse Park."
The first *True-Life Adventure, Seal Island*, is released.

1949 The combination live-action and animated feature *So Dear to My Heart* is released.
Seal Island wins an Academy Award.
Production begins on the film *Treasure Island* in England.
"Kay" Kamen dies in an airplane crash.

1950 The feature animation *Cinderella* is released.
Treasure Island is released.
The first Disney television special, *One Hour in Wonderland*, is viewed by 20 million people.

1951 *Alice in Wonderland* is released.
Work begins on the miniature "Dancing Man" with Buddy Ebsen.
The Walt Disney Christmas Show is on television.

1952 *The Story of Robin Hood and His Merrie Men* is released.
The production of miniatures for Disneylandia begins.
One of the miniature models, "Granny's Cabin," is displayed in Los Angeles.
Walt creates WED Enterprises, his own company, to develop Disneyland.

1953 *Peter Pan* is released.
The live-action *The Sword and the Rose* is released.
WED researches possible locations for an amusement park in California.

Walt and Herb Ryman create sketch of Disneyland for investors.

Walt agrees to create a television program in exchange for funding of Disneyland.

The *True-Life Adventure, The Living Desert*, is released.

1954   *Rob Roy, The Highland Rogue*, a live-action film, is released.

Toot, Whistle, Plunk and Boom, an animation by Ward Kimball, wins an Academy Award.

Opening date for Disneyland is announced and construction begins.

Buena Vista created to distribute Disney films.

The first episode of the television show *Disneyland* is seen by 30 million viewers.

The first *Davy Crockett* episode is aired and starts a cultural craze.

20,000 Leagues under the Sea is released.

1955   An episode of the television show *Disneyland* wins an Emmy.

20,000 Leagues under the Sea wins several Academy Awards.

Walt and Lilly celebrate their 30th wedding anniversary at Disneyland before it opens.

July 17   Disneyland preview opening is broadcast live to 90 million viewers.

July 18   Disneyland opens to the public.

The *Mickey Mouse Club* television program begins.

1956   The *Davy Crockett* series wins and Emmy.

Song of the South and *Bambi* are rereleased.

1957   The television show *Zorro* debuts.

Disneyland continues to expand.

1958   *White Wilderness*, a *True-Life Adventure* is released; it is later criticized for fabricating the lemmings suicide segment.

Research for the location of a second amusement park begins.

1959 The animated feature film *Sleeping Beauty* is released.

The live-action comedy *The Shaggy Dog* is released.
The "Monorail," the "Matterhorn Bobsleds," and the "Submarine Voyage" all open in Disneyland and an "E" ticket ride is defined.

The Mickey Mouse Club television show ends.

1960 Buena Vista releases *Kidnapped*.

Buena Vista releases *Pollyanna*, starring newcomer Hayley Mills.

An elementary school in Marceline, Missouri, is named for Walt.

Walt is Chairman of Pageantry for the Winter Olympics in California and designs the Opening and Closing Ceremonies.

Swiss Family Robinson live-action feature is released.

1961 *One Hundred and One Dalmatians* is released.

The California Institute of the Arts (CalArts) is formed.

Walt Disney's Wonderful World of Color television series begins in full color.

The Parent Trap and *The Absent-Minded Professor* are released, and both are nominated for several Academy Awards.

1962 "Swiss Family Treehouse" opens at Disneyland.

1963 The "Enchanted Tiki Room," with extensive Audio-Animatronics, opens at Disneyland.

Work is underway on several exhibits for the 1964–65 New York World's Fair.

Florida is chosen as the site of the next Disney amusement park.

1964 Walt opens four attractions and an outdoor sculpture at the New York World's Fair.

Abraham Lincoln, the first advanced Audio-Animatronics human figure, appears at the World's Fair in "Great Moments with Mr. Lincoln."

Mary Poppins, a combined animation and live-action feature, is released and earns five Academy Awards.

Walt receives the Presidential Medal of Freedom.

1965   "Great Moments with Mr. Lincoln" opens at Disneyland.

Disneyland has its 50 millionth visitor.

Disney acquires thousands of acres of land in Florida and announces it will build a new park there.

1966   "it's a small world" and "Primeval World," both from the World's Fair, open in Disneyland.

Walt is discovered to have lung cancer and has one lung removed.

December 15   Walt Disney dies.

1971   Disneyland has its 100 millionth visitor.

Walt Disney World opens in Florida.

Roy O. Disney dies.

Chapter 1

COMING FROM THE HEARTLAND

In 1876, the United States of America was celebrating its centennial, the 100th anniversary of its founding. In Philadelphia, the locus of so many historic events in the new nation's establishment, citizens from across the nation were attending the Centennial International Exhibition of 1876, the first world's fair to be held in the continental United States. From May to November of that year, 10 million visitors viewed 30,000 displays from around the world that reflected the official name of the exposition: International Exhibition of Arts, Manufactures, and Products of the Soil and Mine. Like all the world's fairs in the late 19th and early 20th centuries (and Disney's EPCOT later), this one celebrated the concept of progress: industrial, manufacturing, political, cultural, and scientific achievements that put the host country and the participating nations at the forefront of human development.[1] For the United States, it was a chance to take its place next to the powerful and imperial nations of the world. For visitors, it was an opportunity to see the wonders of the world. For an understanding of Walt Disney, it is a foundation that should not be ignored.

The displays ranged from Alexander Graham Bell's new invention, the telephone, to electric lights and meteorites, huge engines, fish,

livestock, typewriters, and a display of photographs by Eadweard Muybridge who later became famous for his explorations of motion through
photographic sequences. The turret of the Civil War warship *The Moni-
tor* was there, as was the arm and torch of the under-construction Statue
of Liberty. Visitors could climb the piece of the Statue of Liberty for 50
cents, the money going to finishing the sculpture which would eventually
be erected 10 years later. The first zippers were displayed, though at the
time they were called clasp lockers. Women had their own hall, which
emphasized more handmade crafts than it did the stirring political issue
of the day: suffrage for women. Susan B. Anthony attempted to read and
distribute the "Declaration of Rights for Women" on the fourth of July at
Independence Hall in downtown Philadelphia, where the official events
were being carried out, but she was prohibited.

The Department of the Interior and the Smithsonian Institution
discussed a display of American Indians as a way of presenting the rem-
nants of the western frontier, which was rapidly changing as the U.S.
government was forcing Indians onto reservations to make the west
safe for white settlers. Indian artifacts were obtained from expeditions
all the way up to Alaska and put in exhibits, but agreement could not
be reached on putting live people on display. While the Smithsonian
representative promised he could provide "the cleanest and finest looking" Indians who spoke English and would bring along a child, dog,
and pony, Congress would not fund the live display. Years later, in Disneyland, Walt did have Indian families as an element in an attraction. While the Philadelphia fair was in full swing, George Armstrong
Custer was defeated and killed after his attempt to battle a coalition of
Plains Indian tribes at the Battle of Little Bighorn in Montana.[2]

Yet after that point, little Indian resistance was mounted, and the
frontier, with its promise of opportunity and freedom for adventurous
Americans, was secure for white settlers and pioneers. At a later world's
fair, in Chicago in 1893, historian Frederick Jackson Turner delivered
a famous paper at the American Historical Association meeting there
in which he presented the importance of the concept of the frontier
in shaping American ideals. Turner described the uniquely American
character or attitude that he thought developed from the push west,
with it promise of free land, great adventures, and freedom of all sorts.
For Turner, and indeed for many Americans for the better part of the

following century, including Walt Disney's own family, this description was an accurate picture of the way pioneering Americans really were. Turner claimed that it was to the frontier that the "American intellect owes its striking characteristics," which he defined as "that coarseness and strength combined with acuteness and inquisitiveness; that practical, inventive turn of mind, quick to find expedients; that masterful grasp of material things, lacking in the artistic but powerful to effect great ends; that restless, nervous energy; that dominant individualism, working for good and for evil, and withal that buoyancy and exuberance which comes with freedom."[3]

This is the America Walt Disney's parents grew up in, and it was an America he would endlessly refer back to whether for nostalgia or realism. The Americans who exhibited these characteristics, which they supposedly acquired by moving west and settling somewhere along the way, were thought to live in the heartland of America, to be the source of its true strength as opposed to the elite and overly intellectual, materialistic, and commercial inhabitants of the East Coast. This belief in and experience of the western frontier is the source of many of the fantastic stories that make up our national folklore and which Walt was to use creatively in his animations, live action films, and theme parks.

The heartland, the middle of the country in so many different ways that Walt Disney would later explore in his many creations, consists of 12 states (Illinois, Indiana, Iowa, Kansas, Michigan, Minnesota, Missouri, Nebraska, North Dakota, Ohio, South Dakota, and Wisconsin) that provided the geographic and population centers of the nation. The largest city in the region is Chicago. Walt Disney's early family history in America is partly a typical story of immigrations and migrations, restless movement across the landscape in search of the elusive promise of America's heart and the American Dream. The 19th century brought both sides of Walt's family, with lots of quirky side trips and unexpected dead ends, together in the heartland of America, in Kansas.

"The name Disney is of French origin and in France was called D'Isigny," states a biographical essay of the Disney family written by Walt's father Elias, probably in 1939.[4] In the essay, which Walt shared with family members, Elias paints a picture of an ancient, noble family dating back to the time of William, Duke of Normandy, and his invasion of Britain in 1066 to claim the throne of England. The date is important because it is used to mark a change in European history and is considered the beginning of the Middle Ages. Interestingly, the events were commemorated in the famous Bayeux Tapestry, a large 230-foot-long embroidered representation and reinterpretation of the events commissioned and displayed by the victors. The tapestry contains panels, somewhat like a comic book, showing the events leading to the conquest, including Halley's comet, seen as a negative omen of the events. The Disney film *Bedknobs and Broomsticks* (1971) used images from the tapestry in the opening credits.

Elias continued his discussion of the ancient history of the Disneys by pointing out that an ancestor was in William's army and as a result was given a large estate where he "lived and reared his children in a good environment, and was classed among the intellectual and well-to-do of that time and age." One of the Disneys went to Ireland according to family tradition, and by Elias's account he married and had a son, also named Elias (but described as Arundel Elias elsewhere) who was Walt's great grandfather. Arundel Elias Disney married Maria Swan, a woman "of good people," said Elias, and they had a son in 1834, Kepple, named, according to Elias, after Admiral Keppel (different spelling), a British sea officer with a somewhat uneven career who fought for the British during the American Revolution.

Arundel Elias Disney, Walt's great-grandfather, was an immigrant from Ireland where he was born in 1801. In 1836, he and his three brothers went to New York and while the brothers stayed in New York and opened a business, Arundel moved to a farm in Canada. He settled near a river, established a sawmill, and provided for his 16 children by making use of the abundant resources in the area. His eldest son was Walt's grandfather, Kepple Disney, who continued farming in Canada after his marriage in 1858 to Mary Richardson, whose family had settled in the area earlier.

Kepple settled on 100 acres of land in the area and he and Mary had 11 children. Their oldest was Elias, born in 1859. Elias remembers their life on the farm in Canada as "a pure and wholesome atmosphere, both physically and morally." But as every biographer of Walt's family has noted, Arundel and then Kepple were dreamers, men with ambitions and wanderlust, inclinations they passed on to their sons and grandsons. Kepple wandered in and out of his home, often in search of an elusive fortune. In 1877 he took his two sons, Elias and Robert, to America in search of gold. They either failed at prospecting or never got there, but Kepple decided to stay in America and purchased 320 acres in Kansas where the family set up a farm.

The harsh and unforgiving state of Kansas became Kepple's home for now, but his son Elias, Walt's father, was soon on the road again, traveling for work and playing the fiddle for cash. Elias eventually returned to Kansas only to hit the rails this time, taking a train trip with Kepple and the neighboring family, the Calls, to check out Florida. In Florida, Elias got to know the Call's daughter, Flora. They later married and Walt Disney was their youngest son.

Flora Call was the girl next door to Elias Disney's family in Kansas. Her family emigrated from England in the 17th century and settled in the northern regions of New York State. Flora's grandfather, like Walt's, headed to California at one point to find gold and traveled the west looking for the right place to settle. Charles Call eventually became a teacher in Ohio but, after some years and several children, moved his family to Kansas, becoming neighbors of the Disneys in the harsh Kansas farmlands and struggling with both farming and the weather.

Married in 1888 on New Year's Day, Walt's parents settled in the wilds of central Florida near Flora's parents. Elias ran an orange grove near the town of Kissimmee, the region where his sons, years later, would return to plan their East Coast park, Disney World. But Florida wasn't right for the restless Elias, so he moved his growing family to Chicago around 1890.

His younger brother Robert was already there, making plans to cash in on the next big thing: the 1893 World Columbian Exposition, which Chicago had just won the rights to stage. This 400th anniversary celebration of the landing of Christopher Columbus in the New World was planned as an extravaganza like the world had never seen. Just a few years earlier, the 1889 Exposition Universelle in Paris had stunned the world with its amazing and exotic displays, including displays of exciting new technologies, examples of strange world cultures, and a stunning new structure, the Eiffel Tower. The United States had staged an unimpressive display of its nation's resources, and the message it conveyed was hardly stirring. Hosting its own world's fair, again, seemed the solution to correcting the bad image of the young nation, which had succeeded previously with the 1876 Centennial exposition.

Chicago battled with New York and Washington, D.C., to be the home of the next world's fair. But the battle seemed nearly impossible for Chicago because right before the turn of the century, the Windy City was a mess. In his study of the fair and its planning, Erik Larson described the nation's second largest city as a place getting progressively dirtier, noisier, meaner, and more dangerous. Noisy vehicles rattled everyday life, and aggressive air pollution turned the skies dark with soot. Trash, sewage, and dead animals shared the streets with rats, flies, gamblers, drunks, murderers, and prostitutes. The place smelled from the slaughter and disposal of 14 million animals a year that were turned into meat to feed the nation. Chicago was seen as a "greedy, hog-slaughtering backwater."[5]

Robert Disney, Walt's uncle, was planning to build a hotel to cater to the visitors who would come to the fair. Eventually 27 million people came to see the exposition and many stayed in the quickly built hotels like Robert's. Elias, on the other hand, was looking for steady work and found it as a carpenter working on world's fair buildings. He also became a contractor, building houses that he sold in Chicago's neighborhoods. The building of the world's fair in Chicago resulted in what came to be called the White City, a beautifully arranged collection of classically designed building, all painted white. Highlighting the achievements of civilization as well as the proof of its progress away from accusations of savagery, the White City was the perfect symbol of both Chicago and America, widely embraced as they both headed toward the 20th century. Instead of being torn between looking back and looking ahead like the 1876 Centennial exposition had been obligated, this fair could go all out in the direction of progress.

After the 19th century turned into the 20th, Walter Elias Disney was born on December 5, 1901. Walt Disney, after he became a famous animator and producer, was often the subject of urban legends, those contemporary mythical stories we use to explain the extraordinary or hard-to-believe. Even this moment of Walt's birth generated two such legends. First, Walt was said to have been named after his parents' pastor, Walter Parr, at the local Congregational Church. Elias had built the church building and was sometimes a substitute preacher there so the families were close. The pastor's wife was pregnant at the same time as Flora, and they supposedly agreed to name both of their boy children Walter Elias. The Disneys did this, but the Parrs waited until they had another boy before they used the same name. Walt's brother Raymond, born in 1890, was almost named Walter and that is the name used to register his birth. The famous Walter Elias Disney, on the other hand, did not have a birth certificate (just a baptismal certificate; not an uncommon practice) and a rumor of his foreign birth and adoption by Elias and Flora was thus born.

Elias and Flora eventually had a total of five children: Herbert born in 1888, Raymond born in 1890, Roy born in 1893, Walter born in 1901, and Ruth born in 1903.

NOTES

1. Free Library of Philadelphia. "Centennial Exhibition Digital Collection." Available at http://libwww.library.phila.gov/CenCol/index. htm. Accessed April 11, 2010.

2. Smithsonian Institution. "Centennial 1876." Available at http:// www.150.si.edu/chap4/four.htm. Accessed April 11, 2010.

3. Turner, Frederick J. "The Significance of the Frontier in American History." *Report of the American Historical Association for 1893*, pp. 199–227. Available at http://xroads.virginia.edu/~HYPER/TURNER/ home.html. Accessed April 11, 2010.

4. Disney, Elias. "Biography of the Disney Family in Canada." 1939. Available at http://www.michaelbarrier.com/Essays/Elias%20Disney/ DisneyFamilyInCanada.html. Accessed April 11, 2010.

5. Larson, Erik. *The Devil in the White City: Murder, Magic, and Madness at the Fair That Changed America*. New York: Crown Publishers, 2003, p. 13.

Chapter 2

DIZ: THE EARLY YEARS

Chicago was just too much for the Disneys and so the family was on the move again when Walt was five. This time they headed to Marceline, Missouri. The small town, with just around 5,000 people at the time, was constructed in the 1880s to be a middle point in the railway journey between Kansas City and Chicago. The Atchison, Topeka, and Santa Fe Railroad ran a rail line that connected the two important cities in Walt's life. Main Street USA in Disneyland is a reduced-scale model of the main street of Marceline. It was designed in this toylike way to entice people into an intimacy with Walt's past, to help them imagine what it was like to live in a rural, early 20th century town.

As a perfect example of rural, small-town America, Marceline held more meaning for Walt than just the midpoint between two bustling metropolises. Marceline became his model of what America was in the past, the foundation upon which his future visions of America could rest. It also provided him with a connection to trains, a connection that was to be played out in many different ways as he grew. Walt, it has been said, was America's bridge between the past and the future, and his stay in Marceline provided one of the key elements of his worldview.[1] To Walt, the past and future were not at odds but were both necessary parts of a coherent picture of a good world.

Today, the city of Marceline Web site features a quote from Walt on its home page: "To tell the truth, more things of importance happened to me in Marceline than have happened since—or are likely to in the future."[2] Although the quote is undated on the Web site (it comes from the 1938 letter cited below), it hints at the way Walt viewed and used his rural hometown throughout his career: as a source of inspiration for the world he wanted to offer the rest of us. When asked in 1938 to write about his impressions of Marceline for the local newspaper, Walt wrote the statement above and then explained that his hometown provided him with first-time experiences like going to the movies or seeing a parade, things that a boy doesn't forget. He added that these first experiences "are of utmost importance in any human being's life."[3]

The Disneys moved to Marceline because Walt's Uncle Robert had property there; once again Robert was helping his brother Elias settle in a new life after Elias looked around for a place to move his family. Elias and Flora settled their family for almost five years on a 45-acre farm. Both Walt and his brother Roy remember the farm life fondly, perhaps because they were too young to have to do their share of the heavy chores. Walt was often described as the family pet because his youth spared him the work and freed him for extensive playtime. There were fields and green hills and streams nearby, and Walt spent time exploring them, learning about nature in a way that would inspire him years later in his nature documentaries.

On the farm they grew wheat, corn, and sorghum; raised pigs, chickens, and cows; grew vegetables; and made butter that sold in the local market. They sold apples in the winter and shared in the harvest activities with their neighbors.[4] The house was without electricity, and water was obtained from a well and a kitchen pump. An outhouse instead of indoor plumbing was the standard for the day. Walt's older brothers, Herbert and Ray, were responsible for most of the farm work. After a few years, Herb and Ray tired of the farm work and left town for a new life in Chicago and then Kansas City when their father demanded that they use their money for the family and not for their personal enjoyment.

During Walt's childhood, his father Elias was alternately described as kind and as stern in all of Walt's biographies and by Walt himself.

The combination is not inconsistent but often Elias's personality is simplistically taken as the root of Walt's later activities in life. But Elias was not simply a stern but caring father. Walt said of him, "He had a violent temper. Yet he was the kindest fellow, and he thought of nothing but his family."[5] Elias was religious but also committed to socialism and at one point in Marceline tried to get his fellow farmers to form a union. He was a musician who fiddled on Sunday (the family did not regularly attend church) and also is always described as somewhat naïve in the ways of the business world. If Walt inherited anything from his father, it is the same complexity of character.

While his father didn't care much for his son's artistic ways, Marceline became the place in Walt's personal history that began his career in cartooning and his love of drawing. The story of how he began drawing has been told in a variety of ways by different people and has been embellished over the years, but the basis of the story is that the simplest encouragement from an adult can set a child on a confident path. As Walt described it in the letter to the city of Marceline, "One of my fondest childhood memories is of Doc Sherwood. He used to encourage me in my drawing, and give me little presents for my efforts. One time I think he must have held a horse of his nearly all day so that I could draw it. Needless to say, the drawing wasn't so hot, but Doc made me think it was tops."[6]

Years later, in an article for the popular newspaper magazine insert *Parade*, in 1956, Walt stated his belief about this kind of support more coherently: "For a child, encouragement from a grown-up can be a thrilling thing with lasting consequence. It can help fix his objectives, give him confidence to drive unswervingly toward his goal, spell the difference between failure and success."[7] By then, the story of the doctor and his horse had taken on the quality of a complete Disney movie script with Walt sketching Dr. Sherwood's beautiful horse and the kind doctor gently praising him as well as buying his drawing with a shiny new quarter. To Walt, both the praise and the money were confirmation that he could become a cartoonist.

Walt and his family also often recounted another story of Walt's early artistic endeavors during which he and Ruth painted the side of the house with tar. Elias, to say the least, was not amused at the time but years later, after Walt became famous for his animations, Elias gave an interview in 1932 in which he described Walt's behavior not as being destructive but as being adventurous and having the "courage of his convictions." Walt, in a letter to his father after seeing the interview, teased his father for his revisionist version of the event. "It seems to me," Walt said in the letter, "that I was always in trouble."[8]

In addition to Doc Sherwood, Walt had extensive encouragement from his Aunt Margaret, Uncle Robert's wife, who, when she visited from Kansas City, praised all his artwork and gave him supplies the family could not afford: papers, pencils, crayons. Other relatives were nearby and gave Walt an extensive network of caring adults. Walt was lucky to have his Uncle Mike working as a train engineer on the railroad from Marceline to Iowa that passed close to their house. Uncle Mike would sometimes stay at the Disney house between trips. Walt's grandmother (Elias's mother) encouraged Walt's mischievous side.

Walt did not go to school until he was almost eight but stayed home and was schooled by his mother Flora until Ruth was old enough to go along. At the Park School in Marceline, Walt was not the most attentive student when both he and Ruth entered the first grade. They only stayed through the second grade. Later, the school, which had 200 students in all grades through high school when Walt, Roy, and Ruth attended, was replaced by a new building named the Walt Disney Elementary School in 1960.

A combination of bad weather, Elias's bad health, and Elias's inexperience with farm work forced the family to sell off the farm and auction off their belongings in 1910. They stayed in town, in Marceline, until the school year was done and then the remaining Disneys—Elias, Flora, Walt, Roy, and Ruth—ended up in Kansas City in 1911 where Walt's Uncle Robert and Aunt Margaret already lived.

The move to Kansas City meant that Walt and his family left behind their difficult but also idyllic life in a small town. The memories of their short time there would affect Walt all his life, from the outhouse and cow udder gags in his cartoons to the design of Disneyland and his *True-Life Adventure* films. Kansas City, a booming town on the Santa Fe Trail that headed west and a central hub for cross-country shipments, was an exciting but also difficult place for Walt. Elias bought a newspaper distribution route and had Roy and Walt work for him, taking most of the receipts for family expenses but giving the boys a small allowance.

They arose at 3:30 every morning to deliver newspapers directly to their customers' doors, then went off to school, and then repeated the work after school with the evening edition. Walt's schoolwork, at the Benton Grammar School, has been uniformly reported as mediocre or undistinguished, with reading and drawing being his favorite activities. He reportedly copied political cartoons and created caricatures that delighted his subjects and in one case earned him a free haircut.[9] He later took several children's Saturday art classes at the Kansas City Art Institute but that was the extent of his early formal training.

Some delightful anecdotes about Walt's antics during these years in Kansas City establish a sense of Walt's developing worldview. In the fourth grade, when assigned to draw flowers, he added human faces on them and was admonished by the teacher.[10] On Lincoln's birthday one year, he came to school dressed as Abe Lincoln and recited the Gettysburg Address for each class in the building, delighting the principal and his teachers.[11] One of the first movies Walt saw was a showing of the silent film, *Snow White and the Seven Dwarfs*, presented as a treat for the local newsboys. One day his principal, finding him drawing instead of paying attention to geography, stated, "Young man, you'll never amount to anything."[12]

Walt became friendly with Walter Pfeiffer and his family, who welcomed Walt into their home and shared their warm, jovial family with him. Walt and Walter took delight in the movies and vaudeville shows and developed their own skits, which they performed for the Pfeiffer family and at school and local amateur nights (as the "Two Walts"). One of their favorite characters was Charlie Chaplin, who was later to become important in Walt's career in Hollywood. They imitated Chaplin and other silent movie stars in their skits.

When Walt turned 15, his father sold the newspaper route and decided to move the family back to Chicago. Elias had another scheme for making money and invested in a jelly factory. He moved to Chicago with Flora and Ruth, but Walt decided to stay with his brothers for the summer and work in Kansas City. Roy had been working on the regional trains selling newspapers, candy, fruit, drinks, and cigarettes. Walt got a similar job, and that summer he was on trains every day for two months. As he described his work as a "news butcher" in later years, "I felt very important wearing a neat blue serge uniform with brass buttons, a peaked cap, and a shiny badge in my lapel. As the train rolled into one station after another I stood beside the conductor on the car steps to enjoy the envious stares of youngsters waiting on the platform."[13] He spent two months traveling the area but made very little money to take to Chicago and his first year of high school.

In the fall of 1917, Walt was enrolled in McKinley High School in Chicago and quickly became the cartoonist for the student magazine. Some of his work addressed the war in Europe, which had begun in 1914. Roy had joined the Navy, and Walt, who was too young for military service, wanted to serve too. In the meantime, Walt developed his cartooning skills further and began considering cartooning as a career possibility. He studied the gags and routines at local vaudeville shows and continued his art education by attending night classes at the Art Institute of Chicago.[14] His sister Ruth remembers that his skills had developed dramatically by this point. When Walt produced an excellent drawing of the human body, one teacher could not believe he had done it himself and thought he had copied it.[15]

Walt continued to work, first in his father's jelly factory, then as a night guard, then at the post office, a job that took him into the summer of 1918. Walt sorted mail and was a substitute deliveryman. He also did extra work making special delivery runs and picking up mail around the city, bringing it into the post office for processing. While doing so, he collected another funny story: one time he forgot to bring in one of the mailbags and left it for two weeks in the stables where he had hung it after rounds with the horse cart.

In September of that year, a bomb exploded in the Chicago Federal Building, set off by antiwar protestors. Walt was leaving work and just missed being hurt by the explosion, which killed several and injured many more. Several days later, Walt and a friend from school found out about the Red Cross American Ambulance Corp, which took 17-year-olds. Walt was still only 16, so he forged his birth certificate to make himself look a year older and talked his mother into signing the appropriate papers. But while he was training for the Ambulance Corp, Walt contracted the flu in an epidemic that eventually killed tens of millions of people worldwide. Walt was driven back to his home by ambulance and nursed back to health by his mother Flora, who also was sick. By the time he got back to his company, they had been shipped out to Europe and on November 11, 1918, the war ended. Walt and his buddies, who had trained to be drivers and mechanics, not soldiers, nevertheless thought their opportunity to go to Europe was lost. But at the last minute Walt and some of the other volunteers got orders to go to France. They sailed from New Jersey to Le Havre, and Walt began a one-year tour of duty with the Red Cross at Evacuation Hospital No. 5 in Paris and a Red Cross canteen in Neufchateau, working as a driver.

Walt, or "Diz" as he was called by friends in high school and overseas, was 17 by now and was introduced to smoking, poker, and dice while overseas. In one session of craps he won 300 dollars and sent part of it home for his mother to save for him. He had been sending home part of his wages and some money he earned doing drawings and other artwork. He had a plan, and it did not involve returning to work in Chicago at the jelly factory or the post office.

NOTES

1. Green, Amy Boothe, and Howard E. Green. *Remembering Walt: Favorite Memories of Walt Disney*. New York: Hyperion, 1999, p. x.

2. City of Marceline. Available at http://www.marceline.org/index. html. Accessed April 11, 2010.

3. Disney, Walt. "The Marceline I Knew." *The Marceline News*, September 2, 1938. Available at http://www.mouseplanet.com/8264/ In_His_Own_Words_Walt_Remembers_Marceline. Accessed April 11, 2010.

4. Thomas, Bob. *Walt Disney: An American Original*. 1st ed. New York: Hyperion, 1994, p. 27.

5. Thomas, Bob. *Building a Company: Roy O. Disney and the Creation of an Entertainment Empire*. New York: Hyperion, 1998, p. 30.

6. Ibid.

7. Disney, Walt. "I'll Always Remember a Country Doctor." *Parade*, September 23, 1956. Available at http://www.mouseplanet.com/8264/ In_His_Own_Words_Walt_Remembers_Marceline. Accessed April 11, 2010.

8. Thomas, Bob. *Building a Company*, p. 20.

9. Thomas, Bob. *Walt Disney*, p. 37.

10. Smith, Dave, and Steven Clark. *Disney: The First 100 Years*. New York: Disney Editions, 2002, p. 7.

11. Ibid., p. 8.

12. Quoted at Mouse Planet, "Walt's School Daze." Available at http://www.mouseplanet.com/8201/Walts_School_Daze. Accessed April 11, 2010.

13. Disney, Walt. "I Have Always Loved Trains." *Railroad Magazine*, October 1965. Available at http://www.mouseplanet.com/8220/Walt_Tells_Why_He_Always_Loved_Trains. Accessed April 11, 2010.

14. Thomas, Bob. *Walt Disney*, p. 43.

15. Gabler, Neal. *Walt Disney: The Triumph of the American Imagination*. New York: Knopf, 2006, p. 33.

Chapter 3

THE ILLUSION OF LIFE

One of best-known urban legends in the United States is about Walt Disney. Urban legends are stories told repeatedly as if they were true and based in fact. They are always secondhand; that is, they did not happen to the person telling the story, and they often have an odd twist to them. The stories are rarely mundane but rather are often scary, disgusting, or just plain weird. Yet somehow they seem plausible, as if they could just possibly be true. Rarely is there a way to verify or debunk an urban legend but that is not the point of these stories: they really are about addressing everyday concerns and puzzles, about helping us make sense of the world.

The urban legend about Walt Disney concerns his death and afterlife. The story, which is actually very simple and has none of the flourishes of many other urban legends, has Walt deciding to have himself frozen after his death in a cryonic chamber. Cryonics, the preservation of living beings through low temperatures with the hopes of revitalizing them in the future, is an unproven technology even today. Back when Walt died, in 1966, it was barely more than a concept. According to the legend, Walt is still frozen, waiting for technology to find a way to revive him.[1] The lovely irony, that Walt was not frozen but rather the opposite, cremated, and was quietly laid to rest, makes the legend all that much more fascinating.

Why do we have this story? Animation, suspended animation, and reanimation are all important themes in 20th-century culture: they address issues of technology and the body, life and death in an era that has extended the former but not conquered the latter. Animation, giving life to inanimate objects and to ideas, is a tremendous power, one that Walt Disney developed in the early parts of the 20th century better than almost anyone else. If anyone deserved to reap the benefits of reanimation, it was Walt Disney.

The former poet laureate of the United States (2001–2003), Billy Collins, explained the kind of inspiration that he could get from animations. Describing classic Warner Bros. cartoons, he said that animations offered "an alternative to the static reality around me that dutifully followed the laws of the physical world (they) presented a flexible, malleable world that defied Newton, a world of such plasticity that anything imaginable was possible." He found fascination in the characters' ability to shape-shift and their "strange freedom" and he noted that "this freedom to transcend the laws of basic physics, to hop around in time and space, and to skip from one dimension to another has long been a crucial aspect of imaginative poetry."[2]

The animation of images has a long history, and each human society seems to have looked for a way to make still images move. Some of the earliest European cave art, dating back nearly 32,000 years, depicts animals in motion who seem to move with flickering fire light. Cave art around the world has similar properties. Sequential images in Egyptian and Mesoamerican books and wall paintings suggest a moving story over time. Shadow puppets (which were to be used again by early animators in the 1920s) depict stories in silhouette animation on screens in many cultures. Puppets and poetry also have for centuries enacted the animation of still objects and images for the purpose of conveying important stories about human life, and each would find a place in Walt Disney's productions. In earlier times and other places, these animated images were holy, or magic. By the time animation came to the motion picture screen, they were no longer specifically associated with religions, but they did still represent a belief system: the belief in the ability of the artist or the technology to make lifeless things come alive or to impossibly experience metamorphosis or to have odd abilities.

The history of the animated film before Walt Disney is not just about the technological steps that made Walt's work possible. It is also about the continuities from the past, about ways of animating ideas, dreams, fantasies, and other worlds that would be a central component of all Walt's work. It was about harnessing or embracing the magic that has been evident throughout human history. This is what Walt was able to do, first with his hybrid live action/cartoon films and later with his celebrated animations. It was a concept he was committed to through his live-action movies and into his development of Disneyland and exhibits at the New York World's Fair.

There were thousands of animated films before Walt and his collaborator, cartoonist Ubbe Iwwerks (later he changed his name to Ub Iwerks), entered the stage in the 1920s, and it is hard to place the moment when the first animated cartoon showed up, but some notable examples help set the stage. Interest in the depiction of motion through sequential photography was exemplified by Eadweard Muybridge in his animal locomotion images from the 1870s. Muybridge was hired by the governor of California, Leland Stanford, to prove that a horse's feet were off the ground at some point in a gallop.

The year 1895 is usually set as the date of the birth of the motion picture and 1907 is often stated as the beginning of animation techniques, although experimentations began with the very first movies. J. Stuart Blackton and Albert E. Smith are credited with being among the first animators when they used stop motion to move objects around a room that looked like they were moved by ghosts in *The Haunted Hotel*. Others, including Georges Méliès in France and Edwin S. Porter in America, used similar techniques in their early films. Emile Cohl in Paris created 250 animated films between 1908 and 1921 using techniques that anticipated Disney: cutouts, moving drawings, fluid motion, "lightning drawing" (speeding up a hand drawing a picture), translating comic strip characters to film, and the representations of fantastic worlds.[3]

In *The Enchanted Drawing* (1900), Blackton interacts with a drawing of a man's face that he has made, and the face reacts to things the artist does to it. *Humorous Phases of Funny Faces* (1906) is entirely animated drawings and one of the first of its kind. Winsor McCay's 1914 *Gertie the Dinosaur* showed smooth animal animation and his 1911 *Little Nemo*, created with 4,000 drawings, showed innovative character motion.[4] One of the most noted animators before Walt was Max Fleischer who invented the Rotoscope (patented in 1915), a machine that projects images onto a glass plate that can then be traced by an artist. This was used to capture more realistic motion for animation because it used a motion picture of real actions for the artist to copy. The Disney production team used rotoscoping in *Snow White and the Seven Dwarfs* (1937) years later. Fleischer's studio also created KoKo the Clown, Betty Boop, and Popeye; the Fleischer and Disney studios were rivals in the 1930s and didn't actually meet until 1956.

Another technological development that preceded Walt was the development of animation cels, transparent films that could be placed on backgrounds and photographed. The patent was given in 1914 to John Bray based on the work of Earl Hurd in his production studio. In 1920, the publication of the first book to describe all the animation techniques currently in use by movie studios would provide the link between Walt and Ub Iwerks and these earlier productions. The book, *Animated Cartoons: How They Are Made, Their Origin and Development* by Edwin G. Lutz set the standard for animated works for years to come. Walt and Ub got hold of a copy of the book and used it as a guide, as their bible, for their early works together.

It's important to know that all these things came before Walt Disney because he is sometimes incorrectly credited with inventing animation. This does not, in any way, take away from Walt's contributions to animation but just shows he was building on the framework set in place by others. So the stage Walt Disney stepped onto when he started animating his drawings was set, but the script that was to enact his remarkable story was still missing. It also must be remembered that animation is usually a collaborative process requiring several people in the early years and a veritable "factory" later on. Some people criticize Walt for not being the one who actually drew all the pictures, but Walt's talents and skill were really in putting a project together, getting ideas out of his head and into the hands of his artists. In his early animations, Walt did some of his own drawings and camera work, but he soon developed a more collaborative process.

Technical know-how is not necessarily the most important quality in an artist who is trying to appeal to mass audiences, anthropologist Hortense Powdermaker once observed in her study of Hollywood in the 1940s. What the artist really needs to understand is how to "interpret man to himself," to help people understand the world around them in terms that make sense and seem to arise from life itself. This is the quality that Walt Disney had, even if he did not actually have the drawing skills needed to make his later characters like Snow White or Mickey and Minnie or Bambi come alive.[5]

When Walt returned from his work with the Red Cross in France, he was still only 17, but he had done a little more artwork while overseas, drawing menus and posters for the Red Cross canteen, decorating footlockers and soldier's jackets, and creating fake souvenirs of German sniper helmets that he and a fellow entrepreneur sold to American troops. He also drew cartoons that he sent off, hoping they would be published in American magazines, but they were not accepted. By the time he left the Red Cross, he had saved 500 dollars, which would come in handy when he wanted to become an artist full-time.

Walt moved back to Kansas City from Chicago in 1919 after refusing to work in a jelly factory at a job his father had arranged. He told his father he wanted to be an artist and submitted an application as a cartoonist to the *Kansas City Star* but was rejected. Walt and Ub Iwerks met in the fall of 1919 when both were working for the Gray Advertising Company at the Pesmen-Rubin Art Studio, a Kansas City commercial art studio that produced ads for local businesses, both in print and to be shown in the local movie theatre. Walt got the job by showing some cartoon work he did in France. He did preliminary layout work that was completed by more seasoned artists. But the work was just temporary and after the holidays, Walt and Ub were laid off.

They decided to form their own commercial art company, using some of Walt's Red Cross savings for supplies. The company, "Iwwerks-Disney Commercial Artists," was just one month old when Walt saw an ad in the newspaper for a job that he couldn't resist: as an artist doing cartoons. Walt got the job with the Kansas City Slide Company (later called the Kansas City Film Ad Company), and Ub was left with "Iwwerks-Disney," which folded two months later. Ub was hired, at Walt's recommendation, by the same firm that now employed Walt at

40 dollars a week. They began working on animated advertisements for local businesses, using cutout, jointed figures (like the earlier shadow puppets) to make animated shorts that were shown in the local movie houses.

They moved away from cutouts after encountering Lutz's book and his description of different animation techniques. Lutz described all technologies from flipbooks to various machines designed to display or project a sequence of images. He also defined all the basics of animation: drawings that change slightly from one image to the next, boards with pegs that align each drawing, and the term to define this new artistic endeavor: animator. For Lutz this was a man of "many accomplishments" including a sense of humor, managerial skills, the ability to "grasp pedagogical principles," and an "untiring and courageous worker" who was not cowed by the prospect of doing thousands of drawings.[6] Lutz illustrated the way the human body moves and the steps of animal locomotion (borrowed directly from Muybridge) as well as animating objects, using symbols, and showing emotions. Walt also looked closely at Muybridge's work, obtaining copies of his motion studies and using them to improve his animation.

Walt borrowed a camera and began experimenting with these many animation forms in a makeshift studio set up in his brother's garage. After he completed a short film, he took it over to the manager of one of the theatres owned by Frank Newman, who was considered an important distributor and exhibitor of motion pictures in the Midwest. He convinced the local theatre manager, Milton Feld, to pay him to produce a regular series of cartoons. Feld agreed, but the price Walt negotiated with him merely covered the cost of supplies, so he didn't make any money from them, but he did build his experience and his reputation.

Walt called the cartoons "Newman Laugh-O-grams" and produced a series of political lampoons of Kansas City as well as special cartoons requested by Feld, including one that warned people not to read the title cards in the silent films out loud. Walt's hand (actually a cutout picture of his hand) in one of the cartoons does a lightning drawing like the ones many early animators experimented with. This was one example of a trend across the country in which locally produced short films played before the feature film. Only a sample reel of Walt's work for Newman has survived. It shows several odd titles including one called "Kansas City's spring clean-up," which questions the efforts of the city to get rid of criminals, riff-raff, and corrupt police, and another that shows Kansas City girls rolling down their stockings.[7]

Walt was still working days at the Kansas City Slide Company and he suggested that they produce cartoons as well as ads to sell to the local theatres, but his boss had no interest. So, after six months, Walt had produced a short animated film that he decided to use to develop his own animation company. He had hired several boys, for no pay but in exchange for instruction in cartooning (a strategy he repeated for years in every company he owned), to complete his first story: a retelling of *Little Red Riding Hood*. Walt had been influenced by this time by the animated shorts of Paul Terry, who reworked Aesop's tales starting in 1921. In 1922, Walt Disney released his first animated cartoon and the credit on *Little Red Riding Hood* read "Cartooned by Walt. Disney."

The story set the pattern of Disney animation that was to come: it is a traditional fairy tale with a contemporary twist. Little Red Riding Hood was a girl who drove a car. She had a cat (somewhat resembling the popular Felix the Cat who debuted in 1919 and who later reappeared in the *Alice* comedies as Julius the Cat) who is armed with a rifle that he uses to shoot holes in the doughnuts Red's mother is making. The doughnuts are for Grandma, and her mother calls Red with some dancing notes, a theme that recurs in numerous Disney works. Red's car is fueled by a dog running behind it, trying to catch a string of sausages. The wolf is a man driving a fancy car that he shrinks and puts in his pocket when he reaches Grandma's house. When he and Red fight inside the house, we don't see them coming to blows, but we see the house come alive, jumping and bulging with the fight. An airplane flies by, hooks the house, and flips it over. Red is rescued and the wolf/man is dumped in a lake.

All the other fairy tales in the series featured similar updating, something that Walt was going to be criticized for years later. Cinderella, for example, had a heroine who was a flapper, and the all-important ball featured a Charleston rather than a classic waltz with the Prince. At the time, however, they were not considered inappropriate and, indeed, many silent films of the era reworked and often spoofed time-honored stories and themes. More significantly, the films all had a story and the animation, while filled with the usual cartoon gags, also showed the importance of storytelling that was to make Walt's work so significant.

Walt was known for his visual gags, which he developed during this time period and used over and over again just like everyone else did. Gags, visual and linguistic jokes or puns, or in the case of animations, breaks in the logic of the world, were supposed to inject humor into the animations and were thought by distributors to be their biggest draw. Walt's gags in *Little Red Riding Hood* (a dog pulling a car, shrinking and pocketing an automobile), like many of those in animation, played with what was possible and what was impossible. Walt Disney is quoted as saying about animation, "Animation can explain whatever the mind of man can conceive."[8] If Walt was just developing his unique vision at this time but had not yet achieved a unique style, certainly his mind was already conceiving things others had not, and this would lead to his next big project.

The completed *Little Red Riding Hood* film gave Walt the confidence to quit his job and incorporate his animation company as Laugh-O-gram Films in May 1922. He had 15,000 dollars from several dozen investors and set up shop with Ub Iwerks again as well as five other animators and a salesman. The salesman took Walt's work to New York and returned with a 100 dollar deposit on a deal: 11,000 dollars for six cartoons, each around six or seven minutes. With *Little Red Riding Hood* done, they started work on *Cinderella, Jack and the Beanstalk, Goldilocks and the Three Bears, Puss in Boots,* and *The Four Musicians of Bremen*, a Grimm's fairy tale not as well known as the others today.

Walt's staff was young and excited to be working in this new medium, but there wasn't always enough money to pay them. Walt used the company's animation camera to shoot newsreel footage and baby pictures to make ends meet, but eventually everyone left the company because the promised fee from New York for the short cartoons, which were completed, was never paid. The distribution company had gone bankrupt. Walt was alone and broke, living in the offices of the animation company and owing money all over town, when he got a job making an educational film for a dentist. *Tommy Tucker's Tooth* earned Walt 500 dollars, was Walt's first educational film, and put him back in business, this time to make something really different and, he hoped, marketable.

Walt came up with an idea for combining live action and cartoons, but his approach was a twist on what other artists had already attempted with, for example, lightning drawings, where they appeared on screen as the creators of the animations shown. Instead of cartoons being part of the real world, the real world would enter the comic world and at least some of the action would take place in an imagined, animated world drawn by hand. This was attempted by Winsor McCay briefly in *Gertie the Dinosaur* when the artist steps into Gerti's drawn world and takes a ride on her back. It was also a popular technique of Max Fleischer's *Out of the Inkwell* series to have humans interact with the animated clown Koko. Walt's idea eventually developed into a series of 56 full reel films (about 10 minutes each) about the adventures of a girl named Alice. He started by making a demonstration film called *Alice's Wonderland*. Walt is credited at the beginning of the film with the "scenario and directing" and he is also responsible for having the nerve to initiate such an extravagant project while facing down economic ruin.

In this story, four-year old Alice, played by Virginia Davis, a girl who did work for the ad company, comes up to the real studio Walt worked in, knocks on the door, and asks if she can watch Walt (who is working at his desk: animators are no longer dealing in magic but in the transparent production of moving images) draw the "funnies." What happens next set the *Alice* movie apart, and even all these years later they still seem quite amazing. As she goes around the studio with Walt, he points out several artists' drawing boards that have animated scenes on them, like scenes he had seen in Max Fleischer's films. On one board is a boxing match between a cat and a dog, and all the artists gather around to watch. Alice goes home and falls asleep and then dreams she is on a train that stops in an animated Cartoonland where she is greeted with cheers and a parade. Chased by four animated lions, she jumps off a cliff. The end of the film has been lost.

Part way through making this demonstration of his new animation concept, Walt again ran out of money. Although he had contacted a cartoon distributor in New York, Margaret Winkler, who showed an interest in the *Alice* series but did not advance him any money, he could not deliver the promised films to her. His brother Roy, who was already in California, told him to give up the company and head west. Although all the best work in animation was being done at that time in New York, Walt took Roy's advice. He quickly earned some money by photographing babies, then sold his camera and bought a ticket, first class, on the Santa Fe Railroad, one way, to California.

NOTES

1. Mikkelson, Barbara, and David Mikkelson. "Suspended Animation, 2007." Available at http://www.snopes.com/disney/waltdisn/frozen.asp. Accessed April 11, 2010.

2. Collins, Billy. "Inspired by a Bunny Wabbit." *Wall Street Journal*, June 28, 2008.

3. Crafton, Donald. *Before Mickey: The Animated Film, 1898–1928.* Cambridge, Mass.: MIT Press, 1982, pp. 12–33.

4. *Little Nemo* is available at http://www.youtube.com/watch?v=kcSp2ej2S00&NR=1. Accessed April 11, 2010; other historic animations are also available at YouTube.

5. Powdermaker, Hortense. *Hollywood, the Dream Factory: An Anthropologist Looks at the Movie-Makers.* New York: Little, Brown and Company, 1950.

6. Lutz, Edwin George. *Animated Cartoons: How They Are Made, Their Origin and Development.* New York: C. Scribner's Sons, 1920, pp.57–60.

7. Samples of the Newman Laugh-O-grams can be seen on YouTube at http://www.youtube.com/watch?v=qaknqmbT99c. Accessed April 11, 2010.

8. Smith, Dave, and Steven Clark. *Disney: The First 100 Years.* New York: Disney Editions, 2002, p. 19.

Chapter 4

1923

In 2009, The Walt Disney Company launched a new "fan community," the first official organization devoted to making fans a part of the Disney tradition and thanking them for years of loyalty. The launch, in the heart of the worst economic recession in decades, featured a Web site and glossy magazine with a brand new logo and concept: D23. The introductory, oversized magazine, "Disney twenty-three," showed a picture of Walt on the cover taken in 1923, the year Walt joined his brother Roy in California. Walt is without his trademark moustache and, standing behind a camera, he is looking intently at the camera's subject.

This D23 official fan club is named for that historic moment when Walt decided to head west like so many Americans before him and find his piece of the American Dream. As this official version of Walt's pilgrimage to California states on the inside cover of the D23 commemorative magazine, the adventurous 21-year-old stepped on a train in Kansas City, Missouri, in 1923 with 40 dollars, a cardboard suitcase, some drawing materials, and a copy of his most recent combined animation/live-action movie. Unofficially, he also carried with him to the golden state of California his first bankruptcy and failed animation company, an empty belly from weeks of meager meals, a new pair of shoes, and a healthy dose of optimism. The Golden State developed its mythic quality early, as visitors from Europe, Russia, Mexico and Latin America, and the new American republic wrote about the strange and dramatic land, its resources and beauty in the late 18th and early 19th centuries.[1] Alta California, as it was known to distinguish it from Baja California to the south, was both dry and lush, coastal and mountainous, desert and oasis. The presence of a substantial native population and Spanish missionaries trying to convert them did little to slow the quest by the new Americans to possess the land. This they did after 1846 when the inhabitants of the region rebelled against Mexico and declared their own republic. The Mexican-American War soon broke out, and the Americans annexed California right after. California became a state without slavery in 1850.

Events moved fast in this remarkable land and at the beginning of 1848, the California gold rush was on when gold was discovered in Sutter's Mill, northeast of the current capital of Sacramento. At least 300,000 immigrants came to the state in the following years and many stayed, giving the land a large and diverse population. The gold rush funded the development of the transcontinental railroad, connecting the east and west coasts in 1869, and it is thought to be the source of the California Dream of easy wealth, good luck, ample leisure, natural beauty, and relative freedom from control. Walt Disney's grandfather, father, and uncle gave gold prospecting a try in 1878, long after the most easily accessible gold was gone, but they soon gave up.

California, even today, has a mystique of possibility about it; in 1923 it was absolutely magical because it was becoming the home to the new medium of storytelling: the motion picture. Motion pictures had been invented just a few decades earlier, and the expansion of motion picture technologies in the late 1880s quickly made moving picture shows a popular form of entertainment in the 1890s. By the beginning of the 20th century, several companies had developed the cameras, film, and projectors needed for the motion picture to develop into a widespread form of entertainment. The first studio in Los Angeles was set up in 1909 by William Selig and his Selig Polyscope Company from Chicago. Most of the early studios were not only seeking the great landscapes, lighting, and climate of Southern California, but they were also putting distance between themselves and inventor Thomas Edison, who was trying to control the burgeoning industry with several crucial patents. Selig had made a deal with Edison in 1908 that supposedly settled his legal issues. But Edison's consortium was controlling and the member companies were restricted in how they could produce and distribute their films.

The earliest movies, right after the first demonstrations in public in 1895, were interested in showing off the technology by depicting actual scenes and activities. But once they began recreating and then fabricating scenarios, they entered the realm of fiction. Films that told stories, like the 1903 *The Great Train Robbery* by Edwin Porter, were very popular as were fantastic films like those of Georges Méliès, who experimented with special effects, including those in his famous *A Trip to the Moon / Le Voyage dans la lune* in 1902.

Selig made *The Wonderful Wizard of Oz* in 1910, and this early film shows the extent to which movies had moved early on into the realm of fantasy that would attract Walt Disney to them.[2] Selig's studio, which lasted until 1918, was eventually changed into a zoo (the animals came from the many nature films he made). The large-scale amusement park Selig planned never materialized, but it was an eerie parallel to the park Disney was eventually able to put together several decades later.

California, continuing its long history of independence from the East, was not favorable to patent claims and this made it a better location than many places for refugee film companies. In 1910, another refugee from the East Coast and from Edison, D. W. Griffith and his Biograph Company, shot the first film in Hollywood. Many other productions followed. and permanent studios started popping up the next year. In a few more years, by 1915, most American movies were being made in or near Hollywood. By the 1920s, when Walt Disney arrived, Hollywood area studios were huge production facilities, and they also owned the movie theatres that showed their films.

Remember that before 1895, motion pictures did not exist as a form of entertainment. The most popular form of theatre entertainment in the United States at the end of the 19th century and the beginning of the 20th was vaudeville, a series of usually unrelated acts (singing, dancing, recitation, lectures, comedy, magic, and later movie shorts) attended by mixed audiences of different classes and genders. Drama and musical troupes traveled the country, performing in local opera houses, and Chautauquas, which often featured costumed reenactments of historic moments and characters, were common. The phonograph was a hugely popular invention by Thomas Edison that was put to use bringing music and voice recordings to the nation. Professional sports like baseball and football were just taking shape at the same time that nickelodeons, local theatres that showed movie shorts, were developing all over the country. By 1907, one *Saturday Evening Post* writer estimated that 2 million people a day were visiting the small theatres and many of these patrons were children.[3] That number was to multiply over the next decade as were large cities and large corporations across America. At the same time, inventions like the automobile made Americans increasingly mobile, and entertainment was increasingly commercialized with the expansion of the technologies to deliver shows and activities to the masses through amusement parks, sporting events, inexpensive restaurants, and motion picture theatres.

So when Walt Disney took a train to Los Angeles, California, in 1923, he was entering a world that was just in the process of being formed. It was a world where anything that could be imagined was about to be possible. When he stepped off in California, he began the process that helped him accomplish what practically no one else on the planet had been able to achieve: he became, over time, "the man who made dreams come true." He probably didn't know that at the time, for the power to make dreams come to life, to actualize fantasy, to make the fantastic a reality, to have the imagination acted out before our very eyes, took many years and more than one short reel of film. But for Walt, those brave steps onto and then off a train were crucial because they opened a series of possibilities that quite possibly were available only one place at that moment, in California.

Walt's brother Roy was in California in 1923 trying to recover from a relapse of the contagious lung disease tuberculosis (TB). At the time, TB was treated with rest, good nutrition, and exposure to the fresh air of the outdoors, warm or cold. Antibiotics to treat the disease had not yet been developed. Roy had moved to New Mexico and Arizona first, and then ended up in a veteran's hospital in west Los Angeles. Roy all this time had been sending blank checks to Walt in Kansas City with the offer of up to 30 dollars at a time; Walt often took him up on the offer.

Roy was convinced that Walt, if he stayed in Kansas City, could not survive in the business of making animations. Walt had already been taken by a bad distribution deal, and Roy was certain he would accomplish nothing unless he moved away. Walt, meanwhile, said he was thinking of trying his hand at directing instead of animation, and he was convinced that a Hollywood studio would hire him when he came west. He had experience, after all, with filming newsreels and the completed *Alice* film. Being swindled by a distribution company had soured him on the field of animation. Walt acknowledged his failure and was ready to move on. Or was he?

Walt arrived in California in July 1923, and moved into his Uncle Robert's house. Robert Disney had moved west in 1922, joining many other Midwesterners who made the trek. Walt didn't get a job right away, but he did hang around the movie studio lots all day, watching and learning while pretending he was there to apply for work. He actually did get a job as an extra in a western, but rain delayed the shoot and the extras were recast another day. Walt needed money to pay Uncle Robert room and board, so he planned a new set of joke films to sell to the local theatres. He set up yet another makeshift animation studio and began working on the films.

In the meantime, he sent off a new note to Margaret Winkler, the cartoon distributor in New York. He told her of his move west, the fact that he was establishing a new studio, and that he had the *Alice* films in mind as a series that he would like her to distribute. It was August and Winkler, at just that moment, was losing two of her big cartoon clients: the Felix the Cat franchise and the movies of the *Out of the Inkwell* gang. Walt sent her a copy of *Alice's Wonderland* and while that film was not to be part of the deal (it was still owned by Laugh-O-gram), it did convince her to give him a contract for a series of six films and the possibility of renewals. The price was 1,500 dollars a film, and Walt had to produce one film a month. In October 1923, Walt Disney, Cartoonist (as he stated on his stationery), was back in the animation business.

Walt convinced Roy to leave the Veterans' sanitarium and come work with him in the business that would create the *Alice* films. Walt figured they could make the movies for about 750 dollars each and so see a profit that could be turned back into their work. They established the Disney Brothers Studio and funded their early work with

200 dollars Roy had saved from his pension, 500 dollars that Uncle Robert somewhat reluctantly lent to his nephews, and a 2,500-dollar loan that Roy and Walt's parents, now living in Portland, Oregon, were able to put together by mortgaging their house. Once again, the Disney family stood behind Walt (and now Roy) in attaining his dream. Years later Walt gave a speech in which he talked about Roy's guidance and business help. He explained, "If it hadn't been for my brother I swear I'd have been in jail several times for checks bouncing. I never knew what was in the bank. He kept me on the straight and narrow."[4]

The contract with Margaret Winkler called for the original actress who played Alice, Virginia Davis, to be the star of the series. In order to do this, Virginia and her family had to move to Los Angeles. Walt and Roy offered them 100 dollars a month, and they were on the West Coast in time to film the first project in the contract, *Alice's Day at Sea*. Walt did all the animation for the project while Roy was taught how to run a camera for the live-action sequences. The one-reeler was finished the day after Christmas, and when they received their check, the brothers went on to make the second film, *Alice Hunting in Africa*, followed by a third, *Alice's Spooky Adventure*. Winkler was listed as the producer on the credits as M. J. Winkler Productions. While Winkler accepted the films, she was critical of them, asking for more comedy and bigger laughs, but Walt was already trying to distinguish himself from the other slapstick comedies of the time; he wanted, he wrote to Winkler, to keep the comedies more "dignified."[5]

Winkler was also looking for more animation sequences. Walt had kept them to a minimum because they were more expensive and time-consuming to produce. And, for the first few films, Walt was the animator. In *Alice's Day at Sea*, the animation in the early part of the film is sparse but used very effectively: a clock puts on an angry face when it's alarm is not heeded, and a craggy old sailor tells a story of a giant squid taking down a ship that is simple white lines on a black background.[6] By today's standards it is crude, but in 1920 it was integrated into a delightful storyline better than most animations of the time. Alice then falls asleep while sitting in a boat, and we are once again transported into Cartoonland. The storm sequence of a boat on swelling wave, while repetitive like much of the animation of the times, is wonderfully dimensional (the same sequence is redrawn by Ub Iwerks and used again in *Alice the Whaler* in 1927). When the boat goes down, a live-action Alice emerges under the sea. Fish entertain her, and there are all sorts of gags—fish riding scooters, zoo animal fish, fish traffic (reminiscent of *Finding Nemo* years later), dancing fish—and she only awakens when she is tangled in a net in the boat she is sleeping in.

Alice's Spooky Adventure recalls some of the early animators' use of a haunted-house theme to demonstrate stop-action animation. Alice enters the house to retrieve a ball, and a box is moving around the floor. When plaster from the crumbling house drops on her head, she enters the cartoon world (Alice often is unconscious when she enters Cartoonland). Once again music, even though the film is silent, plays a part in her adventure as it will in many later Disney films. By now Walt has some help with the animation by Rollin Hamilton but is still doing much of it himself; he is also credited with writing, directing, and producing it, with Winkler now listed as the distributor. The cat Julius is introduced (Julius appeared in the unreleased *Alice's Wonderland*) to the audience and appeared in the rest of the films.

The first six one-reelers of the *Alice* series were done by May 1924, and by this point Walt was looking for help with the animation. He contacted Ub Iwerks, who was still working at the Kansas City Film Ad Company. Ub agreed to come to California for 40 dollars a week and arrived shortly afterward. The *Alice* comedies become more and more animated and less and less live action. The contract with Winkler was renewed, only now it was Margaret's new husband who initially withheld some of the money that had been promised to Walt and Roy. The details were worked out, and a total of 57 episodes in the *Alice* series were created over three-and-a-half years by an ever-expanding staff. Several other animators from Kansas City also joined the crew to make *Alice's Wild West Show, Alice and the Dog Catcher, Alice Gets in Dutch, Alice Hunting in Africa,* and many other *Alice* shorts. Perhaps most significantly Walt was developing a reputation in Hollywood for being the producer of quality animations. Reviewers in the trade newspapers found the series novel and fun.

Both Roy and Walt solidified their personal lives as well during this time. Roy had a girlfriend back in Kansas City, Edna Francis, and she had been with him since he left for the war and through all his stays at sanatoria for TB treatments. Edna had even lent Walt money when the Disney brothers needed it, although Roy did not approve of this. And while the brothers worked well together in their studio in 1923 and 1924, they didn't live together in their apartment as smoothly. After yet another disagreement with Walt, Roy decided to marry his girlfriend Edna and set up a real household. His telegram to Edna was positively received, and they were married in April 1925. Walt was the best man, and the maid of honor was a young woman named Lillian Bounds.

Roy and Walt had hired Lillian in the office in January 1924, at 15 dollars a week, and she eventually ended up doing both cel paintings and secretarial work. Lillian Bounds, described as sweet and gentle but also independent, funny, tough, and loving by her family, had come to California from Idaho in 1923 to stay with her sister Hazel. She was the youngest of 10 children, born in 1899, and back in Idaho, her father was a blacksmith and a Federal Marshall on the Nez Perce Indian Reservation where she grew up. It was the Nez Perce (their own name for their tribal group is Nimi'ipuu) who in 1877 conducted one of the last Native American battles with U.S. government troops before they surrendered and moved to this reservation.

There is a Nez Perce myth about a boy who was sad because he was not married. The people called him "Iwapnep Atswitki," or in English, "Cry-because-he-had-no-wife." He found a woman picked out by his grandparents, and the adventures involved in taking her to his family and later taking her back home turned him into a man.[7] Such stories are told, as Walt knew in his work with fairy tales, to explain how the world works. Certainly Lillian Bounds, or "Lilly" as Walt called her, rounded out Walt's life and helped complete his transition to adulthood. Years later Lilly would say of her husband, "Any genius, especially Walt Disney, is wild-eyed and needs a practical family to watch over him."[8]

Lilly initially took the job at the Disney studio because she could walk to it from her sister's house. It must have seemed odd, then, that her boss, Walt, offered to drive her and the other girls home, but he always ended up dropping her off last. The romance blossomed; Walt met Lilly's family after preparing himself by buying a new suit, and they were soon married. The wedding took place in Idaho in July 1925.

After a short honeymoon, Walt was back at work and facing new problems with his distributor, Margaret Winkler's husband Charles Mintz. Mintz claimed that he lost money on every *Alice* comedy delivered to him so far, and Walt complained back that he was not being paid the contractual amount. According to Mintz, Walt "should wholeheartedly be ashamed" of himself while Walt countered with threats of discontinuing the series. When they finally came to an agreement in early 1926, Walt and Roy not only had a new contract for the production of more *Alice* comedies, but they had a share of the rental profits and a stipulation that the rights to any merchandise associated with Alice—including toys, novelties, and comic strips—were the property of the Disneys.[9]

At the same time, the Disney brothers moved their operation to a larger space, hired more help, and changed the name of their production company: it was now "Walt Disney Studio." Apparently both Roy and Walt thought this would sell their pictures better. Walt was no longer animating himself but took on the role of the producer, developing stories, scripts, and early versions of storyboards; creating the gags; supervising the other animators; and defining shots, motion, and characters. Later, animations were roughed out, and previews of the actions were analyzed before final drawings were done. This is a significant step in the history of animation, and it marked the beginning of Walt's greater influence. His vision of what animation could do—create images of things that existed only in the imagination yet which seemed more real than the real world—and how to achieve these effects influence animated work to this day. His production process, in which meetings are held to develop and act out stories, characters are developed and discussed as if they were real beings, and motion is both faithful to reality and fantastic, became the Disney style.

The studio made *Alice* comedies all through 1926 and into 1927, including *Alice in the Alps*, *Alice in the Big League*, *Alice the Whaler*, *Alice Foils the Pirates*, and *Alice the Beach Nut*. Every two weeks or so the expanded team sent Mintz a short animation and Mintz, suspiciously, continued to minimize their efforts, complaining both when the films were late and when they came too early. Three new girls were cast as Alice in the final films in the series as Virginia Davis moved on to other roles.

As the *Alice* series was winding down, Margaret Winkler showed she still had some fingers in the animation game by encouraging Walt to develop the new animated character that her husband had made a deal to develop with Universal Pictures. Since everyone seemed to be acknowledging that there were too many cats on the screens, a simple change to a rabbit was seen as a way to innovate and make new, appealing cartoons. Mintz named the character Oswald, the Lucky Rabbit. Ub Iwerks made some sketches of Oswald as a floppy eared rabbit with a decidedly Mickey Mouse face. Walt sent the sketches on to Mintz who passed them on to Universal for approval. Walt Disney Studio, now finishing with the *Alice* live-action/animation comedies, was moving on to an all-animated series featuring Oswald. Walt and Roy received a contract for 26 cartoons at 2,250 dollars each but with the merchandising rights (including the Oswald Milk Chocolate Frappé Candy Bar and a stencil set for drawing your own Oswald) not going to the Disneys.

No longer, however, were characters copied off of model sheets that Walt drew out to be traced by his animators. Characters that had been developed and become regulars in the *Alice* comedies—anthropomorphic cats, dogs, and mice, and objects that came to life—reappeared as members of the Oswald cast but not just as retreads. They developed into fuller personalities, and this is considered another great contribution of Disney to the world of animated characters. This concept of "personality animation," where characters don't just move but have distinct characteristics that affect what they do and how they interact, became a noted Disney animation characteristic.[10] Each step of this new personality animation required thinking out the logic of the character's world and its capabilities, and while it took some time to develop his personality, Oswald became a prime example of this animation philosophy. This became especially evident in the early Oswald cartoons when, for example, Oswald developed the habit of taking off body parts and using them as props.

Oswald was not just animated by one person. Each animator worked on different parts of the action, being assigned scenes by Walt. Ub Iwerks was noted for his depiction of mechanical objects (especially in *Trolley Troubles* and *The Mechanical Cow*). He worked with Friz Freleng on his assigned films. Another team, with Ham Hamilton (noted for his character pantomimes) and Hugh Harman, was doing a different film at the same time. The animators were given bonuses if their ideas made it into a film and additional bonuses for getting work done on time. The opening credits for all the cartoons read "Universal presents OSWALD The Lucky Rabbit" and "A Winkler Production by Walt Disney."

Oswald the Lucky Rabbit was born at a time when the major studios were interested in distributing animations, and Universal did an ad campaign even before the first story was completed. When Disney's first animated Oswald short, *Poor Papa,* was sent to Mintz and Universal in April 1927, however, they both hated it. Mintz and Universal said that Oswald didn't look right, that he was too old, too fat, and that the premise of the story was wrong, repetitious, and not funny (in *Poor Papa,* Oswald has to fight off storks delivering numerous babies). Poor Papa was not released immediately, and it wasn't until the next try, *Trolley Troubles,* that Oswald was successful. The movie received favorable reviews and wider distribution than Disney had been used to; the series brought welcome attention to the Walt Disney Studio and the series of 26 films was produced throughout 1927, although some were not released until 1928. Ads by Universal for the Oswald cartoons called Oswald "the most consistently screened cartoon figure of the present day," and "originality in theme and treatment are the ingredients responsible for Oswald's great success."

Most reports of the world of animation in the 1920s and '30s indicate that this was a vicious and cutthroat game, resulting in internal discord and external feuds between individual artists and whole companies. Animators fought over credit for creating characters and complained about working conditions. Walt experienced this turbulent work situation in his own studio, and individual artists left when they couldn't work with his approach. But after the one-year contract on the Oswald cartoons was up, Walt learned a lesson about the world of animation that he would never forget.

Walt decided to go to New York in February 1928 to talk to Mintz in person about a new contract for the Oswald cartoons. He and Lilly took a train there to meet with the distributor. Mintz's brother-in-law, Margaret's brother George, had been at Walt's studio several times during the production of the first few Oswald films, and George's discussions with the animators raised suspicions that he was up to something. In New York, Mintz offered Walt not a raise for the next set of Oswald films but a reduction in his rate. Mintz pointed out that he, not Walt, owned the Oswald character and that Walt should sign because Walt's animators had already signed with Mintz. Walt, finding this hard to believe, called Roy who discovered that this was true. All the animators, except Ub Iwerks, the young men he had trained in Kansas City and then hired in California, were turning their backs on him and signing with Mintz to continue the production of the Oswald series. Although negotiations continued, Walt felt Mintz wanted too much control of the entire project, so he walked away from Oswald the Lucky Rabbit. The Disney corporation did not regain rights to the Oswald cartoons until 2006.

It was Hugh Harman who led the defection of the animators from Disney to Mintz. Many explanations have been given for this move. Some see it as disloyalty on the part of Harman and the other animators who were with Walt from the beginning. Others say that Hugh and Rudolph Ising (one of Walt's early animators and a longtime friend from Kansas City) never made a secret of their desire to run their own production company, and this was simply an opportunity to do that. Still others claim that Walt's tyrannical attitude in the studio drove away his otherwise loyal employees. Some attribute it to the jealousy of animators who did the work but whose names were not as well known as Walt Disney's.

Walt and Lilly got on the train and headed back to California with a stopover in Kansas City. But what happens next is one of the most mythological elements of Walt Disney's story. Walt had decided to create a new cartoon series with a new character, a mouse, because of his fondness for the mice that occupied his office in Kansas City. As Walt remembers it, this thought came to him somewhere west of the Mississippi. And Lilly, on that train or some time later, in response to early sketches or upon hearing the first script, apparently objected to the character's name, Mortimer. To her it was horrible and despite Walt's insistence on Mortimer, she continued to object. So, at some point, Walt Disney said, "How about Mickey? Mickey Mouse." A legend, and an American icon, were born.

NOTES

1. Starr, Kevin. *Americans and the California Dream, 1850–1915*. New York: Oxford University Press, 1986, pp. 3–7.

2. The film is available for download at http://www.archive.org/details/The_Wonderful_Wizard_of_Oz. Accessed April 11, 2010.

3. Patterson, Joseph Medill. "The Nickelodeons: The Poor Man's Elementary Course in the Drama." *Saturday Evening Post*, November 23, 1907. Available at http://thenostalgialeague.com/olmag/nickel.htm. Accessed April 11, 2010.

4. Thomas, Bob. *Building a Company: Roy O. Disney and the Creation of an Entertainment Empire*. New York: Hyperion, 1998, p. 5.

5. Thomas, Bob. *Walt Disney: An American Original*. 1st ed. New York: Hyperion, 1994, p. 74.

6. *Alice's Day at Sea* can be seen at http://www.youtube.com/watch?v=YE1F1UMJ0m0. Accessed April 11, 2010.

7. Judson, Katharine B. *Myths and Legends of the Pacific Northwest*. Chicago: A. C. McClurg & Co., 1912, p. 86. Available at http://www.secstate.wa.gov/history/publications_view_pdf.aspx?i=SL_judsonmyths/SL_judsonmyths.pdf. Accessed April 11, 2010.

8. Disney, Lillian, as told to Isabella Taves. "I Lived with a Genius." *McCall's*, February 1953.

9. Thomas, Bob. *Walt Disney*, p. 80.

10. Merritt, Russell, and J. B. Kaufman. *Walt in Wonderland: The Silent Films of Walt Disney*. Baltimore: Johns Hopkins University Press, 2000, p. 81.

Chapter 5

BUILDING A BETTER
MOUSE/TRAP

Up until 1927, almost all movies, whether using cartoon characters or live actors, were silent. Movie theatres usually had musical accompaniment in the form of a pianist, an organist, or sometimes an entire orchestra, but any dialogue or commentary was displayed on title cards. There were a few experiments in adding sound to movies before 1927, but most of these involved short bits of unsynchronized dialogue or music. There were a few attempts at recording entire movie scores, but these were simply replacements for in-house musicians.

Then, in October 1927, a remarkable event marked the beginning of the end for the silent film era. A movie called *The Jazz Singer*, featuring a popular vaudeville-style performer called Al Jolson, opened in New York. Jolson was considered the "World's Greatest Entertainer" at the time and he was famous for his stage show, which featured him telling jokes and singing in blackface, with his lips painted white and his hands sporting white gloves. Blackface was common on the vaudeville stage and used by both blacks and whites as a form of masking. While it is quite unthinkable today for someone to do that because of the association of that style of performing with racial insensitivity, there seems to be every indication that Jolson was actually very active in promoting racial equality. So the fact that Jolson appeared in *The Jazz Singer* in blackface was not what made the movie remarkable; what made that moment so important in the history of the movies was what happened when Jolson opened his mouth to sing: sound came out. *The Jazz Singer* featured both recorded dialogue and musical numbers, both synchronized with the image. Audiences at the premiere apparently went wild for the movie, and it had a long run in theatres. The "talkies" were born and Hollywood movie production was changed forever.

Several months later, in March 1928, Walt and Lilly were returning from New York after their fateful visit with Charles Mintz. But even though Walt had begun developing a new character, Mickey Mouse, that would replace Oswald the Lucky Rabbit, he was not yet taking the dramatic step that would make his career. But the change was not far off. When Walt got back to Los Angeles, he and Ub Iwerks worked on the character of Mickey, defining his shape and his personality. For decades later, debates raged about just who created Mickey, who was responsible for this cultural phenomenon. A 1931 article in *Time* magazine about cartoons of the era stated that cartoonist Walter Disney "gives his collaborators no publicity. He is the originator and so far as the world knows the sole creator of Mickey Mouse's doings."[1]

Never again was Walt not the complete owner of something he created. Reflecting on the events with Mintz, Walt registered the Mickey Mouse trademark in May 1928 and copyrighted the Mickey cartoons. Trademarks are words, names, or symbols that are used to distinguish one company from another. A trademark, unlike a copyright, can be extended indefinitely. Copyright is a legal protection given to original works of "authorship" that are "fixed" or presented in some medium. Ideas, concepts, or procedures for producing this work cannot, however, be copyrighted. Copyright is both a protection of the creator and a protection of the public's right to eventually access works with the idea of fostering creativity and encouraging additional creations. The owner of a copyright has exclusive rights to reproduce, perform, or distribute that work for what is supposed to be a limited amount of time. Then it reverts to the public domain, meaning that anyone can reproduce and use the work in any way they wish. Walt learned this lesson the hard way when Charles Mintz took the Oswald character that he had created but for which Mintz had obtained the appropriate copyright. Mintz, in his new studio's work with Krazy Kat, was successfully sued by the Disneys because Krazy Kat was developed to look remarkably like Mickey!

In 1998, when Mickey was 70 years old, and more than 30 years after Walt's death, the California congressman, Sonny Bono, gave Mickey and his corporate owners a present. He helped develop a bill in the U.S. House of Representatives that extended the copyright protection of Mickey Mouse, a protection that was about to lapse. The bill that was later passed, after his death, is known as the Sonny Bono Copyright Term Extension Act (named this because Bono died in a skiing accident before its final approval). But it is also known as the Mickey Mouse Protection Act because many people saw it as another example of the Disney corporation forcing this additional protection on its most important character. The new bill gave corporations that had registered their original product between 1923 and 1963 a total of 95 years of protection from the date of publication. For the first versions of Mickey, this meant that his potential move into the public domain, where anyone could use his image and his films, was pushed back at least to 2023. The U.S. Supreme Court (in *Eldred v. Ashcroft*) affirmed the constitutionality of the bill in 2003.

The protected-by-copyright Mickey was, from the start, a unique persona, a character with an identifiable set of characteristics and an individuality that distinguished him from other cartoon characters. True, his mousey forefathers showed up in the *Alice* cartoons and he and Oswald had a lot in common. But he was soon to become so different from his contemporaries—Koko the Clown, Krazy Kat, and Paul Terry's *Aesop's Fables*—that Mickey would soon be known all over the world: in German he was "Michael Maus," in French "Michel Souris," in Spanish Miguel "Ratonocito," in Japanese "Miki Kuchi" or "Mik-kii Ma-u-su," in Italy "Topolino," in Finland "Mikki Hiiri."

But his characteristics and Walt's protection of him were not the only thing that created Mickey's fame; it was what happened when he puckered his lips to whistle in his theatrical debut, in the first sound synchronized cartoon called *Steamboat Willie*. However, the first Mickey cartoon actually created, a traditional silent one, was called *Plane Crazy*, and it celebrated the transatlantic flight of Charles Lindberg that had been completed in May 1927. *Plane Crazy* was drawn and animated by Ub Iwerks. Ub had to work on Mickey's cartoons in secret because the rest of the crew in Walt's studio were still finishing up the old Oswald contract before they left Walt for good. In May 1928, Walt showed *Plane Crazy* to distributors, but there was no interest in it. Cartoons were no longer the novelty they had been, and many theatres no longer showed them. Ub and Walt, meanwhile, were still working on two other Mickey cartoons, *The Gallopin' Gaucho* and *Steamboat Willie*, and continued to develop these stories.

Both these movies were spoofs of, as well as homages to, great silent motion picture stars and their work. *The Gallopin' Gaucho* celebrated the romantic adventure movies of Douglas Fairbanks, which were extremely popular with audiences in the 20s. Fairbanks helped form Hollywood as well as the Academy of Motion Picture Arts and Sciences (which began giving out Oscars in 1929). He was known for his roles in *The Mark of Zorro* (1920) and *Robin Hood* (1922) and in *The Three Musketeers* (1921), *The Thief of Baghdad* (1924), and *The Black Pirate* (1926). In 1927 he released a film called *The Gaucho*, which was set in South America (a region that became important to Walt later in his career).

Steamboat Willie was an undisguised borrowing from the film *Steamboat Bill, Jr.* (released May, 1928) which starred one of the most talented and popular silent comedians, Buster Keaton. Keaton was known for his sad, deadpan face and his innovative physical comedy. As a model for animators of cartoon characters, he was a rich resource of action and reactions that found their way into many of the popular cartoons of the day. Keaton learned his trade in vaudeville, and he and his family shared a stage with Harry Houdini at the turn of the century, just as Walt Disney was born. Keaton was one of the Disney studio's silent film influences, along with Charlie Chaplin, Harry Langdon, and Mack Sennett's Keystone Kops.

Ub animated *Steamboat Willie* in a few weeks in the summer of 1928, working alone and creating up to 700 drawings a day. Walt's significant contribution, besides developing Mickey's character and the story for *Steamboat Willie*, was getting the first fully synchronized sound animated cartoon actually made. It was not easy because no one had really done what he wanted to do. Right from the start, he wanted music, dialogue, and sound effects used creatively, almost as another actor in the story. His music didn't just accompany the action; it helped create the story and tied together the competing elements. His sound effects were clever and witty and verbalized gags in a way that was similar to the stage performers like Al Jolson. What that meant was that sound was no longer just something in the background; it was now essential to the story. It's hard for us to imagine today what a dramatic change this was in motion pictures.

Walt worked with Ub and his new studio hire, Wilfred Jackson, on the timing of the scenes, creating more detailed exposure sheets and story guidelines than ever before. He took these and the finished animation to New York in September and started searching for a studio that could do what seemed to have eluded other cartoon makers: getting the sound perfectly synchronized. Walt was shown how other cartoonists, his competitors, were also trying to experiment with sound, but he wasn't impressed by what he saw. Walt eventually went to a company run by a man named Patrick Powers, who had (some say dishonestly) muscled his way into sound recording for films. After several tries with an orchestra they came up with a satisfactory soundtrack. But his efforts at getting Steamboat Willie into theatres were not automatically rewarded as distributors were not anxious either to book a cartoon or to get involved with Powers's sound system. The distribution companies also wanted to own the Mickey cartoons rather than just distribute them, but Walt had learned the lesson about keeping ownership of his creation. Pat Powers found a local theatre to run *Steamboat Willie* and set an opening date. He and Walt also signed a contract for Walt's sound cartoons.[2]

November 18, 1928, is considered the birthday of Mickey Mouse (although in the past, several dates between September and December have been used).[3] On that date, the first Mickey Mouse sound cartoon that Walt Disney could get released in theatres was seen by audiences at the Colony Theatre in New York. It played for 13 days along with a movie called *Gang War* (which also had elements of sound), and a performance by an orchestra and singers. The *New York Times* reviewed it briefly:

On the same program is the first sound cartoon, produced by Walter Disney, creator of "Oswald the Rabbit." This current film is called "Steamboat Willie," and it introduces a new cartoon character, henceforth to be known as "Mickey Mouse." It is an ingenious piece of work with a good deal of fun. It growls, whines, squeaks and makes various other sounds that add to its mirthful quality.[4]

Steamboat Willie, Mickey Mouse's adventure as a steamboat pilot, starts with music as the credits are shown. Then a steam paddleboat appears, spewing black smoke rings, each of which is accompanied by a puff as the sound of the turning paddlewheel and music fills the background. Whistles on the top of the boat toot, perfectly synchronized, as they stretch and squash to show which one is making the noise. Mickey doesn't speak but makes noises in reaction to the gruff treatment from the steamboat captain.

All the effects that were developed over the past 25 years in cartoon animation—bodies stretching out of shape and then reforming, animals talking, objects acting like humans—all now had their magic enhanced by sound that seemed natural and drawn directly from the screen. When a goat eats a musical score, Mickey and Minnie turn it into a hurdy-gurdy, a mechanical music player. Everything on the boat is then used to create music: pots, spoons, a washboard, and a trash can are played like drums. Animals are put to use as musical instruments: a cat is stepped on to create screeches; baby pigs suckling have their tails pulled for squeals; the mama pig is played like an accordion; and a cow is used as a xylophone.

While waiting for *Steamboat Willie* to open, Walt worked in New York on the recording of sound for *Plane Crazy* and *The Gallopin' Gaucho*, assuming or hoping that Mickey would be a big hit. Due to the work of the publicist who owned the theatre it debuted in, the movie got attention in the trade newspapers and was well reviewed. With his contract from Pat Powers, Walt was able to go back home to California, begin expanding his staff, and make more cartoons. The contract with Powers, however, was not as favorable to Walt as he had assumed. When he had to renegotiate it in a year, it became clear that Powers had attempted to manipulate him just like the other distributors. In a series of complicated negotiations and deals, Walt was able to pay off Powers and sign a more favorable deal with Columbia Pictures for both

Mickey cartoons and a new series Walt and his team were developing, *Silly Symphony* cartoons.

The *Silly Symphonies* took advantage of the sound revolution and created a new type of cartoon. First, the music was written by Walt's Kansas City friend and composer, Carl Stalling, and then the animators got to interpret the music with their visual gags. They had no recurring characters, and this freedom let the animator use their imaginations. By this point, the animation of cartoons had become much more of a group process with the animation pipeline now set by Walt's design. After the initial meetings about the story and the gags, the main animator draws the key frames, or most important changing points in the action. "In-between" artists then fill in the action that takes place between these key points. As always, the inkers finish the job by filling in the outlines and adding shading. The work is then turned over to the photographers.

Ub Iwerks was given the responsibility of directing the *Silly Symphonies* and for the first one, *The Skeleton Dance*, he did nearly all the animation himself. In *The Skeleton Dance*, Ub created actions and images that had not been seen much before. The skeletons belied their bony structure and were loose and floppy as they cavorted in a graveyard. They moved in and out of the camera, filling it up with their gruesome faces. While not an easy sell because it seemed too spooky to some distributors, *The Skeleton Dance* was released in August 1929. It became the first in a series of 75 *Silly Symphony* cartoons that were popular at the same time that Mickey was. Columbia Pictures advertised the series as the "Greatest Talking Picture Novelty Ever Screened!"

Back in New York, Walt was still working out a deal with Pat Powers. But Powers, like Charles Mintz before him, dealt Walt a blow that was both personal and all business. In a telegram back home to Lilly, Walt had said that the New York animators took their hats off to Ub and admired his work. Powers more than admired him; he thought Ub should work for him directly and not through Walt. Powers lured Ub Iwerks away from the Disney studio, offering Ub his own cartoon series and studio. Walt found out while he was negotiating the contract with Powers. Ub left early in 1930, and Carl Stalling decided to leave at the same time, citing his inability to work with Walt.

The reasons for Iwerks leaving Walt after so many years are tangled and will probably never be fully understood. In the telegram from Roy to Walt that announced Ub's resignation, Roy states: "gives his reason personal differences with you." In a film biography created by his granddaughter, Ub's reasons are generally stated as, "Walt began to control the artistic direction of the company in ways Ub didn't expect." Ub was described as wanting to follow his own pursuits and regain his artistic independence. Still in Walt's shadow, he was feeling the strain of the expanded production schedule and the increasingly regimented rules for producing both Mickey cartoons and the *Silly Symphonies* on time and under budget.[5] Whether it was Ub's annoyance at Walt's criticisms and control of his work, or his failure to be credited with the creation of Mickey Mouse, or artistic differences even as Ub was working on the new *Silly Symphonies* series, Ub moved over to Powers's side and the Disneys bought out his interest in their production company. By all accounts, Walt was devastated.

But by then, Mickey had taken off—in fact, he had become famous—a cultural phenomenon to rival the popular live movie stars of the day. The reasons for this are varied and decades of analysts, beginning in the 1930s, have delighted in picking the Mickey Mouse phenomenon apart. Biographer Neal Gabler summarizes many of these, showing that Mickey was considered, among other things: an "animated surrogate" for either Charlie Chaplin or Douglas Fairbanks; a symbol of America's positive spirit, survival instincts, altruism, and freedom; a representation of traditional values and the desire for order; a model of what was right and normal; a narcotic for adults who escape with him into a world of fantasy and childishness. Mickey's circular design was supposedly reassuring and designed to subliminally elicit love from his primitive human worshipers.

Mickey's connection to Walt was noted by many: he was considered Walt's on-screen presence, a way for Walt to express his "personal mythology of trial and triumph," according to Gabler. Gabler elaborates that "Mickey engaged in fantasy only to have it punctured by reality. ... He was acting out the central tension of Walt Disney's life." He was, Gabler concluded in a psychological and philosophical vein, "the eternal promise of cheerful solipsism," a character, like Walt, who could "always make things right in his head" even if on the ground of reality they were far from perfect.[6] For others the connection was kinder and suggested that both Mickey and Walt were eternal optimists and also very sure of themselves. The connection became hard to deny when Mickey started speaking in his films because Walt became his voice and continued doing Mickey's famous high voice until 1947. In the 1948 edition of *Who's Who in Hollywood*, an essay attributed to Walt includes these affectionate comments about Mickey:

> Mickey could never be a rat.
>
> He had become a hero in the eyes of his audiences, especially the youngsters. Mickey could do no wrong. I could never attribute any meanness or callow traits to him. We kept him lovable although ludicrous in the blundering heroics. And that's the way he remained, despite any outside influences.
>
> I often find myself surprised at what has been said about our redoubtable little Mickey, who was never really a mouse, not yet wholly a man—although always recognizably human.
>
> Psycho-analysts have probed him. Wise men have pondered him. Columnists have kidded him. Admirers have saluted him. The League of Nations gave him a special medal as a symbol of international good will. Hitler was infuriated by him and thunderingly forbade his people to wear the then popular Mickey Mouse lapel button in place of the Swastika.
>
> But all we ever intended for him was that he should make people everywhere chuckle with him and at him.
>
> The life and ventures of Mickey Mouse have been closely bound up with my own personal and professional life. It is understandable that I should have sentimental attachment for the little personage who played so big a part in the course of Disney Productions and who has been so happily accepted as an amusing friend wherever films are shown around the world.[7]

Mickey, then, doesn't stand in for or represent any one thing. The power of an icon like Mickey is his flexibility, the ease with which he can be attached to any idea or any feeling, as if he were so easy to get, to understand. It is the mark of a good icon that he seems to satisfy the very requirements each situated critic demands. If kids needed him to be funny and silly, he was. If adults needed him to be suggestive and a good anarchist, he could be seen that way too. Walt usually dismissed most of this analysis, and his explanations were usually simple and to the point: Mickey satisfied audiences who could see something of themselves or their situation in his on-screen antics, however fantastical they were. Mickey was also a corporate icon and through the years he became something of a model for children, a role that ended up limiting his adventures and behavior after a while.

The Mickey of the 1930s stopped being a troublemaker and became a bit less naughty, but it wasn't his fault: censorship had hit the movies. Both religious and secular groups had some objections to the content of the movies from the beginning. By the 1920s, that concern got formalized into a set of voluntary industry regulations that later were called the Hays Code, named after the man hired by the studios to oversee it. In 1934 the Catholic Church established its own code to guide Catholics in their choice of movies, with calls to boycott unacceptable ones. The Hays office responded in kind and its guidelines began to be enforced. Each movie, including cartoons, now needed a seal of approval that was posted with the film's advertisements. Without the seal, most theatres would not show a film that, according to the code, "lowered the moral standards of those who see it."

Mickey animated cartoons were censored a bit for Mickey's exuberant behavior but mostly for their elaborate use of cow udders, a funny set of gags that go all the way back to the *Alice* cartoons. The udder gags, coming from the Kansas City rural background of all of Walt's early animators, consisted of udders that swayed violently back and forth, stretched and squashed into every form, squirted milk when they were grabbed, and were just plain huge. Both Ub and Walt loved barnyard jokes, which continued in the studio's production for years. In *Plane Crazy* (animated by Ub Iwerks), Mickey is chasing a cow in his plane and the cow's huge udder eventually overwhelms the plane, filling the screen with two teats hanging down.

Walt's studio was putting out one new Mickey cartoon and a new *Silly Symphony* just about every month. It got to the point when people just expected to see a new Mickey on the bill. A new expression developed: "What! No Mickey Mouse?" to express the surprise when a new cartoon wasn't a part of the show. The saying developed into a song by composer and lyricist Irving Caesar: "What! No Mickey Mouse? (What Kind of Party Is This?)" and became a saying in the culture to indicate an unmet expectation or disappointment.

Mickey was considered one of the best symbols of all things American in the years before World War II (even before his movies were cleaned up), and he earned Walt an honorary Academy Award in 1932, a remarkable achievement since it had been only a few years since Mickey's birth. The award stated, "To Walt Disney for the creation of 'Mickey Mouse.'" The League of Nations (an organization of different countries, forerunner to the United Nations, which was concerned with peace and human rights) awarded Walt its highest honor in 1935 for Mickey and the good will he spread around the earth.

In 1929 Mickey was just beginning to become an important cultural experience. A theatre in California started holding Mickey Mouse Club meetings on Saturday afternoons. This became formalized in theatres across the nation and within a few years one million kids (aged up to seventh grade) were members of the club in hundreds of locations. The kids—sometimes lined up around the block to get into the theatres—elected officers, participated in rituals, sang songs, acted in talent shows, viewed cartoons, watched magic shows, entered contests (including cracker eating), had yo-yo demonstrations, and participated in patriotic and "citizen-making" activities. It was all a lot of good clean fun. The members had badges and membership cards. They viewed serials (westerns and Rin Tin Tin) whose cliffhangers got them coming back the next week. There was a Mickey Mouse Club song (Minnie's Yoo Hoo song from the cartoons) and members (the Mickey Mice boys and Minnie Mice girls) gave a hearty Mickey Mouse Club yell:

Handy! Dandy!
Sweet as candy!
Happy kids are we!
Eenie! Ickie!
Minnie! Mickey!
M-O-U-S-E!

And they recited the Mickey Mouse Creed: "I will be a square shooter in my home, in school, on the playground, wherever I may be. I will be truthful and honorable and strive always to make myself a better and more useful citizen. I will respect my elders and help the aged, the helpless and children smaller than myself. In short, I will be a good American." The rituals and activities created a community of kids who were devoted to Mickey and who created a market for Mickey merchandise. Walt had been the member of a youth group after the war called Demolay, which guided boys and young men; it too conducted rituals that created a sense of community. Walt credits the organization with teaching him the basic principles of life.[8]

"If you build a better mousetrap the world will beat a path to your door," or so the saying goes. For many people who are critical of the current Disney corporation and how it grew into a merchandising giant, what came next for Roy and Walt was just the beginning of that mousetrap. In October 1929, the stock market crashed in the United States and within a few years the country had entered a time of financial woe that came to be known as the Great Depression. Unemployment was high and businesses and banks were failing. The Great Depression persisted in the United States until the country's entry into World War II in December 1941.

Mickey Mouse, however, got credited with saving a few companies, and it was not just through the cartoons and the many animators now employed to create them. Roy and Walt expanded into Mickey merchandise, casually at first and then with the same care and foresight that kept them in business so long. While he was in New York in 1929, a man approached Walt and asked him for permission to put Mickey on some children's writing tablets. Walt agreed, and the price was 300 dollars. In California, a local woman, Charlotte Clark, began making dolls based on Mickey Mouse and went to the studio to get permission to sell them. Walt liked them and set her up with the equipment needed to manufacture them. At that point they were used for promotions, as giveaways.[9] A toy manufacturer, George Borgfeldt & Co., made many different Minnie and Mickey character articles, including Mickey parade canes, hand puppets, rattles, sparklers, handkerchiefs, ashtrays, and toy tea sets under a license Roy signed in 1930.

Mickey and his adventures also became a comic strip in newspapers across the country. In January 1930, the first strip featuring "The World Famous Movie Character Mickey Mouse" was licensed and published in newspapers; the story was "Lost on a Desert Island." The early stories were similar to the animations, with Mickey and Minnie in simple scenarios in stories written by Walt and illustrated by Ub Iwerks or his assistants. When Ub left, Walt stopped writing the stories, and the job of making Mickey a staple in the daily newspapers went to a rookie animator, Floyd Gottfredson. Gottfredson changed Mickey into an adventurer and wrote and drew his comic strip for 45 years. In these long serialized stories, Mickey and his friends traveled all over the world, into mythology, and through time, often searching for treasure or battling great villains like the Phantom Blot or Peg-Leg Pete. During World War II, Mickey was working as a secret agent or fighting the Nazis or having problems with Minnie. An entire universe of minor characters developed over the years in this extensive and complex world.

While the first comic strip was in 1930, the first comic book came out in 1940. Many newspaper comic strips were made into comic books in the 1930s and 1940s as a way to repurpose the popular strips and give them an extended life. Mickey strips were made into the *Mickey Mouse Magazine*. This later became *Walt Disney's Comics and Stories* and featured more original work. By 1942, during the height of World War II and its paper shortages, the comics were selling over a million copies and came out every month. Bear in mind that comic books were coming under heavy scrutiny during this time period and by the postwar period they were under attack for making aggression and violence acceptable and supposedly causing juvenile delinquency. Even Disney comics were not safe from scrutiny. At one professional conference of psychotherapists led by the noted anticomic activist Frederic Wertham, a speaker complained about the violence taking place "between little anthropomorphic animals: gouging, twisting, tearing, and mutilating one another—Disney style."[10] By the mid-1950s, congressional hearings on violent and gory crime, romance, and horror comic books led to bans or difficulties in distribution. Disney comics, generally considered more wholesome despite the noted animal violence, fared better than most during this period of self-censorship.

Comic books became an extensive production for the Disney company, but Walt and Roy also licensed the production of the comics rather than doing it all in-house. The comic books were produced all over the world in many languages. Comic books were published for most of the animations and later the live feature films and *True-Life Adventures*. Other comics addressed aspects of Disneyland and science and technology associated with one of Disneyland's original science-oriented worlds, Tomorrowland. The *Silly Symphonies* were made into comic books as well. By the 1950s, 3 million Disney comics were sold each month.

If the online Disney comic book database put together by international aficionados of Disney comics (called INDUCKS) is correct, there are more than 198,200 Disney comic stories available in 108,476 publications.[11] It would be impossible to view all of these, but a sampling will give a sense of how extensive this form of Disney magic has spread around the world. In one early comic strip example, Mickey wants to be a musician and buys a piccolo, which he carries out of the music store in a bass fiddle case so he doesn't look "sissified." Mickey fails as a musician, and the music that he wrote is eaten by a goat (like in *Steamboat Willie*), but the goat dies because the music is so bad.

Through the strips and the comic books, Walt's artists introduced and developed other famous Disney characters. Most notable are the stories by artist Carl Barks, who created an entire duck-filled universe surrounding the characters of Donald Duck and Scrooge McDuck. In a 1959 Huey, Dewey, and Louie strip that appears at the end of the Donald Duck comic book, the duck nephews of Donald are in school. In this short strip, Daisy, Donald's sometime-girlfriend, is teaching the little duck boys how to spell cat. With her back to them as she writes on the board, the boys send paper airplanes flying out the open window. Daisy catches them and marches them to the principal's office. She is horrified, but the boys are delighted when Donald, lounging in his principal's chair, is also throwing paper airplanes out the window.[12] The theme of the adult in authority who gives in to his childish, innocent ways recurs in many Disney stories but was one focus of the criticism of comic book foes.

The merchandise, the comic strips, and later books and comic books were bringing in some money now to the studio, but Roy and Walt were not entirely satisfied with the character merchandise and its marketing. So when a Kansas City marketer, Herman "Kay" Kamen, contacted them, they agreed to discuss possible alternatives. He had gained a reputation for his work with Hal Roach's *Our Gang* series of movies, and he featured the kids from the series on furniture, toys, and pencil boxes. The Disneys met Kamen and put him in charge of signing more products but also maintaining the quality of the merchandise bearing the Disney name.

The general public could now buy Mickey sports equipment, paint sets, dolls and dollhouses, puzzles, tents, beach toys, soap, candy, umbrellas, and socks, shoes, and hats. Kamen expanded the licensing beyond the kid's market. Now there were not only stuffed and ceramic Mickeys and Minnies but also high quality watches, blankets, clocks, toothbrushes, tableware, holiday decorations, and clothing. Hundreds of products appeared, all feeding revenues into the studio. Kamen signed a deal with a reputable but nearly bankrupt maker of timepieces and had them create what is today a highly prized collectible: the Ingersoll Mickey Mouse watch (by the merged company Ingersoll-Waterbury Clock Company). The watch was introduced at the 1933 Chicago World's Fair, which celebrated a "Century of Progress" at the city's centennial. The sale of 2.5 million watches in two years allowed Ingersoll-Waterbury to survive and even expand in the middle of the Great Depression.

The same thing happened to the Lionel Corporation, which made train sets and nearly went under as unemployment increased and discretionary spending decreased in the country. With their Mickey and Minnie windup handcar, they were able to stay out of bankruptcy, selling 250,000 or more units and attracting buyers back to their more expensive train line. Newspapers of the time credited Mickey with saving both companies. Profits from the merchandise were turned back to the studio, which physically expanded, hired more staff, and created many more successful cartoons. Kamen was earning the studio about $200,000 a year in royalties from merchandise and other rights (like sheet music), and this became a Hollywood practice that today is recognized as a standard way to market a film.[13]

Why was Mickey merchandise (and later character tie-ins) so popular? Was it simply that Kamen was a good salesman or that Walt's crew was making irresistible cartoons and the manufacturers made appealing toys and clothes and other props? Just as Mickey merchandise was taking off, speculation about what made people buy products that featured a goofy looking mouse started appearing. An article in the *New York Times Magazine* summarized the ideas: either Mickey satisfies our fantasies of defying authority, or is an example of how the little guy can win against giants. Perhaps, they speculated, it is because Mickey "declares a nine-minute moratorium on the debt we owe to the iron facts of life. He suspends the rules of common sense and correct deportment and all other carping, conventional laws, including the law of gravity, that hold us down and circumscribe our existence and cramp our style." He is not, others have suggested, an animal or merely a cartoon; he is a personality, and perhaps as close as we get to the concept of an "Everyman." Rejecting these high-minded explanations, however, they fall back on the idea that Mickey is, simply very funny and not very complex, decent, and well marketed.[14]

Perhaps a more social explanation does this amazing proliferation of merchandise more justice. Material culture—things, tangible objects, souvenirs—provide a way to connect a person to an experience, a place, a feeling, a memory, or a time. These souvenirs or mementos communicate something about an event or place, help store the memories, or are useful as reminders of the experience. Years after a trip to Disneyland, a stuffed Mickey or a set of mouse ears can bridge time and elicit wonderful stories. As gifts, Disney associated products connect the giver and receiver as all gifts do: in a relationship that very likely involves exchanges of other sorts, of stories and photos and memories. Thinking of corporate produced merchandise only as a commodity (which is at the heart of much Disney criticism) strips it of all the social relations and human connections that attach to it during its circulations.

Walt and Roy Disney, very early on, especially with the marketing of Mickey Mouse, understood that people wanted some material culture to go along with their experiences of the imagination. We can't ever be sure where this confidence in such a largely untested idea came from. Mickey merchandise was not only a set of products that the Disney corporation produced in order to continue and expand its revenue streams. Character merchandise created a sense of community and a loyalty that can still be seen in the generations that grew up on Mickey cartoons, games, music, books, and comics.

Material culture has a way of defining an era, as archaeologists have long known when they dig up the material remains of past civilizations. In 5,000 or so years, some future archaeologists are expected to open a time capsule that was buried at the 1939 World's Fair in New York.

In the capsule they will find many things that reflect everyday life in America during the time of the Great Depression. Included in the time capsule, for future earthlings to contemplate, are two Disney items. In the collection of "Articles of Common Use," specifically those "For the Pleasure, Use, and Education of Children," is a "Mickey-Mouse child's cup of plastic material." In the category of "How Information is Disseminated Among Us" are two Disney comic strips from September 18, 1938, "Mother Pluto" and "Mickey Mouse." During this time, as the war that was already beginning in Europe, Mickey's place in American life was firm, even as Walt moved on to his next steps forward in animated storytelling: color cartoons and an animated feature-length movie.

NOTES

1. "Cinema: Regulated Rodent." *Time*, February 16, 1931.

2. Barrier, Michael. *The Animated Man: A Life of Walt Disney*. Berkeley: University of California Press, 2007, p. 61.

3. See http://www.mouseplanet.com/8168/Walt_Disney_Celebrates_Mickeys_Birthday. Accessed April 11, 2010.

4. Hall, Mordaunt. "The Screen; More Gang Fights." *New York Times*, November 19, 1928.

5. Iwerks, Leslie. *The Hand Behind the Mouse: The Ub Iwerks Story*. United States: Buena Vista Pictures Distribution, 1999.

6. Gabler, Neal. *Walt Disney: The Triumph of the American Imagination*. 1st ed. New York: Knopf, 2006, pp. 154–55.

7. Disney, Walt. "What Mickey Means to Me." *Who's Who in Hollywood*. Vol. 1, No. 3, April–June 1948, Al Delacorte, ed. New York: Dell Publishing Co. Available at http://www.mouseplanet.com/8168/Walt_Disney_Celebrates_Mickeys_Birthday. Accessed April 11, 2010.

8. Disney, Walt. "Deeds Rather Than Words," in *Faith Is a Star*, Roland Gammon, New York: E. P. Dutton and Co., 1963.

9. Smith, Dave, and Steven Clark. *Disney: The First 100 Years*. New York: Disney Editions, 2002, p. 28.

10. Legman, Gerson. "The Comic Books and the Public." *American Journal of Psychotherapy*. Vol. 2, No. 3, 1948, p. 418.

11. INDUCKS. Available at http://coa.inducks.org/. Accessed April 11, 2010. Another Disney comics database is called OUTDUCKS. Available at http://Outducks.org/. Accessed April 11, 2010.

12. Walt Disney Productions. *Walt Disney's Donald Duck*. Vol. 67. Edited by Walt Disney Productions: Dell Publishing Co., Inc., 1959.

13. Gabler, p. 198.

14. Robbins, L. H. "Mickey Mouse Emerges as Economist." *New York Times Magazine*, March 10, 1935, p. 8.

Chapter 6

THE GREAT DEPRESSION
OR WALT'S FOLLY?

In 1956, Walt Disney gave a series of interviews to the *Saturday Evening Post*, a popular weekly magazine. Published in eight installments, the series was presented as if it were written by Walt's then grown daughter, Diane. The series was, in fact, written by writer Pete Martin, and the purpose of both the interview and the writing credit was so that Diane could be paid the 100,000 dollars for the series in order to buy a house.

In the fifth article, Walt talked about the 1930s, and he revealed that his working too hard and worrying too much about the business led to what he and Diane called his "crack-up," or a "nervous breakdown" sometime in 1931.[1] In the 1950s, this was an amazing revelation. Discussions of mental conditions were not as common as they are today and for one of the world's most famous men to make this admission, just a year after the opening of Disneyland, was unusual. The term "nervous breakdown" is not an official term from clinical psychology but a popular phrase. It uses the metaphor that says the human body and/or mind is a machine that will break or get worn from too much stress or work. The point was to connect the sad and angry feelings the patient had to some condition of his body and to use that idea to fix things.

As Walt himself described it, "I simply went to pieces. I kept expecting more from my artists than they were giving me, and all I did all day long was pound, pound, pound. Costs were going up. Somehow, each new picture we finished cost more to make than we figured it would earn; so I cracked up." He continued that he became irritable, couldn't sleep, and would break into tears. "I was in an emotional tailspin," his machine metaphor continued. Putting a positive spin even on this breakdown, the article stated, "Part of his trouble was an acute attack of perfectionism." From his doctor Walt got the advice to relax, exercise, and develop a few hobbies.[2]

There were high points and low points along the way to the breakdown. Walt often said he felt betrayed by Ub Iwerks and Carl Stalling in early 1930 as well as the manipulations of Pat Powers. At the same time, Roy and Edna had their son, Roy Edward in January 1930 (Roy E. Disney was to play a large role in the later Disney Company). Lilly, on the other hand, experienced her first of several miscarriages in the summer of 1931. Mickey was successful, but Walt had new ideas for animation that demanded more staff and bigger facilities, all of which ate up the studio's profits.

In October 1931, Walt and Lilly boarded a train heading east and ended up in Washington, D.C., where they viewed the national monuments. Then they headed to Florida to catch a boat for Cuba. Cuba in the 1930s was a tourist destination, and ferries and cruise ships from Florida landed weekly. Tourists came seeking beaches, horseracing, casinos, and the Cuban music, food, and dance popularized in American books, movies, and restaurants. Lilly and Walt took their return cruise through the Panama Canal. When they returned several weeks later, Walt took his doctor's advice and started different forms of physical activity. He tried many things: swimming, calisthenics, horseback riding, ice-skating, wrestling, boxing, dancing, golf, and polo. Polo became a passion, and Walt eventually owned several polo ponies. Explaining this seeming extravagance to his parents, he noted somewhat apologetically, "Don't fall over dead when I tell you I have six polo ponies now. But after all, it's my only sin—I don't gamble or go out and spend money on other people's wives or anything like that, so I guess it's okay."[3] Walt and some of his animators played at the fields at Will Roger's ranch, which still today features polo matches that include Hollywood celebrities.

*U.S. cartoonist Walt Disney poses with his wife
Lillian and one of his creations, Mickey Mouse, on
the roof of Grosvenor House in London, June 12,
1935. The couple were in London on a honeymoon, although they had been married for 10 years.
(AP Photo)*

Roy wrote a letter to his parents worrying that Walt, even after the trip, was still moody. Walt, however, describes his complete recovery in the *Saturday Evening Post* series. But there were still problems to deal with. Lilly suffered another miscarriage before she had a success-ful pregnancy that resulted in the birth of their first daughter, Diane Marie, in December 1933. Years later, Diane would confirm that her mother was hesitant at first to have children. Walt wanted lots of them, but Lilly saw how hard the other women in her family struggled to raise children. But Walt and Lilly now had a comfortable house, cars, and clothing. Their family grew as they added a daughter through adop-tion, Sharon Mae, in the beginning of 1937. Walt was by all accounts a doting father and became a welcome playmate for his children. Fears of kidnapping (the famous Lindberg baby kidnapping and murder had just taken place in 1932) apparently kept Diane and her sister Sharon close to home and somewhat isolated from other kids.[4]

Back in the studio, things had changed again as the result of two new, innovative *Silly Symphony* cartoons. These two projects made possible both the idea of and the completion of the project that came to be known as "Walt's Folly." First, in 1932, the studio had just finished a particularly nice *Silly Symphony* called *Flowers and Trees*. It had the same basic premise of music (in this case several classical pieces) providing structure for a short sequence of creative animation. The story was about two trees in love. Walt and Roy had been looking into the availability of color for their cartoons and were particularly interested in the Technicolor full-color process. Until that time, most movies were in black and white, with a few exceptions, including Douglas Fairbanks's *The Black Pirate* in 1926. Color processes had been introduced, but the colors were not always acceptable, and Technicolor seemed the best at the time. Roy and Walt negotiated a two-year exclusive contract for the use of Technicolor for cartoons, which meant that all their competitors would have to wait to get their first high-quality cartoons released.

Producing a color cartoon would be more expensive than a black-and-white version, but distribution was even more expensive because of the color prints. Nevertheless, Walt took the completed *Flowers and Trees* and had it reinked in color. In July 1932, the latest *Silly Symphony* was released, becoming the first cartoon in full color, and setting the stage for all the releases to follow. Audiences loved the color effects and the expressive characters, the result of changes in the studio staff. Some of the animators had been taking art lessons, and after *Flowers and Trees* they started life-drawing classes and observations of real motion. These in-studio classes led years later to Walt and Roy's development of Cal Arts (California Institute of the Arts), which combined the Los Angeles Conservatory of Music and the Chouinard Art Institute, which had provided the early lessons at the in-house Disney animation school.

In May 1933, the Walt Disney Studio released another *Silly Symphony* called *Three Little Pigs*. Walt rewrote the familiar fairy tale story to have the focus of the tale be the sympathetic three pigs and the threatening big bad wolf. He had the characters speak in rhyme and many famous sayings came out of the movie including, "I'll huff and I'll puff and I'll blow your house in!" and "Not by the hair on our chinny-chin-chin." Walt's notes on the story reveal his priorities at the time. The pigs were to be clothed (although two of the pigs had only short jackets and no pants) and have human characteristics and live in human houses. The story was to have depth and feeling and a moral about hard work.[5] The animators were starting to get Walt's idea that the characters needed to exhibit personality and real human emotions. *Three Little Pigs* won the 1934 Oscar for "Best Short Subject, Cartoons," the first year the category existed.

The cartoon ran for months in some theatres and reaped several million dollars at the box office. Some people later came to interpret *Three Little Pigs* as Walt's statement on the Great Depression, but he dismissed this idea. The song from the cartoon, "Who's Afraid of the

Here are the three little pigs in person, shown December 20, 1933. They were responsible for all the sound effects in Walt Disney's animated cartoon. Walt Disney, the creator, is at left, and the others, left to right, are Dorothy Compton, second pig; Pinto Colvig, third pig and "Big Bad Wolf"; and Mary Moder, the first pig. Frank Churchill, who wrote and played the score, is at right. (AP Photo)

Big Bad Wolf," became popular all over the country, played on the radio and by orchestras. The pigs and the wolf became a cultural reference point, used to describe everything from sports plays to the economy to politics.[6]

The project that many in Hollywood called "Disney's folly" came after these two advances in cartoon animation. Walt's role at this point in the studio's dynamics was as a producer, the one who coordinates and oversees all the different aspects of the project. As he described it for the *New York Times*, "I do not draw, write music or contribute most of the gags and ideas seen in our pictures. My work is largely to supervise, to select and shape material, to coordinate and direct the efforts of our staff."[7] He developed the idea of the storyboard even further, making it a standard way to lay out a movie that is used to this day. Walt's storyboards, however, came alive well before they were animated. He was known for acting out each scene of the story, taking on the role of each and every character, giving them voices and demonstrating their unique bodily characteristics. He supervised the "sweatbox," which was the small viewing room in which the early sketches—before they were inked—were reviewed.

The studio itself had physically expanded with new rooms for all the different parts of the increasingly complex projects. Some animators from the period talk about the relaxed atmosphere in the studio, its pleasant colors and loose structure, the bonuses for work done on time, the outdoor athletics and casual clothing, and Walt's changed supervisory style, which was less harsh. Others recall that later in this period, Walt sent memos to artists criticizing their work and work habits. In December 1935, Walt wrote an extensive memo that describes what he expected from his animation staff as it was embarking on a wonderful new project. Earlier in the year, Walt had requested that his art instructor, Don Graham, review the portfolios of, and hire, several hundred artists to do the work on the next project.

In the memo to Graham, Walt explained the characteristics of a good animator and how he expected Graham to train both new hires and old hands to meet these expectations:

The list should start with the animator's ability to draw; then, ability to visualize action, breaking it down into drawings and analyze the movement & mechanics of the action. From this point, we would come to his ability to caricature action—to take a natural human action and see the exaggerated funny side of it—to anticipate the effect or illusion created in the mind of the person viewing that action. It is important also for the animator to be able to study sensation and to feel the force behind sensation, in order to project that sensation. Along with this, the animator should know what creates laughter—why do things appeal to people as being funny.[8]

Walt also explained his general philosophy, which had developed through the years and which was now to be applied to the new project coming up:

The first duty of the cartoon is not to picture or duplicate real action or things as they actually happen, but give a caricature of life and action—to picture on screen things that have run thru the imagination of the audience to bring to life dream fantasies and imaginative fancies that we have all thought of during our lives or have had pictured to us in various forms during our lives. Also to caricature things of life as it is today or make fantasies of things we think today.[9]

In the four years from 1934 to 1937, the Walt Disney Studios continued their production of both Mickey Mouse and *Silly Symphony* cartoons. Donald Duck, Pluto the dog, and Goofy were introduced and appeared together with Mickey in several shorts. But the project that was to demonstrate forever that the history of Walt Disney is really the story of the birth and maturation of the art of animation was the feature-length cartoon *Snow White and the Seven Dwarfs*. Feature animation: the concept was almost unheard of in the 1930s. While today we expect quite a few feature animations to be released each year, before *Snow White* it was thought that audiences, as much as they liked Mickey and all the other cartoons that were around, would not sit through a long cartoon. Most cartoons were still one-reelers, about nine minutes, and while Disney cartoons were exhibiting characters and stories, a feature-length cartoon could be 10 reels or more.

The road to *Snow White* started with a series of ideas about expanding the studio's income and range. The short films did not bring in enough money, and it was the merchandising that kept the studio afloat. Since fees for films were based on the length of the film, a longer cartoon would get higher fees. Movie theatres were showing double features now to lure Depression-era audiences in, and there was not enough demand for short cartoons as a result. In the middle of the Great Depression, the Disney studio survived and by 1934 had close to 200 staff, many of them trained by the Disney art program, and this was an investment they did not want to lose.

Walt was also always looking ahead to new ideas for using the capabilities of animation, and the move in recent years toward more realistic- or naturalistic-looking movement placed him in a good position to consider a story that let him prove that animation could do what live action only dreamed of. The studio was already in discussions to produce a film based on a book about Bambi, a deer, but it did not proceed very far. The art lessons that had casually started for the animators a few years earlier were expanded to a full-time school. Many of the artists hired had no animation background and the studio ended up training them. Don Graham, who had done earlier classes, was put in charge of the school and taught the artists how to draw and animate in the Disney style, including from live models and animals at the zoo.[10]

The style came to be known as the "illusion of life." Two of the animators, Frank Thomas and Ollie Johnston, eventually published the ideas they all utilized in a book that is still considered the best one available about the animation process. The illusion of life that was introduced so dramatically in *Snow White* carried over into theme park development, Audio-Animatronics, nature films, and live features as well as computer animation well after Walt's death.

The basic concept behind this kind of animation (as opposed to the surreal actions carried out by, say, Road Runner) is that the animated characters actually "think and make decisions and act of their own volition," and those acts reference real life even if they don't completely adhere to reality.[11] The idea was to base the animation on reality but then push it beyond that, to what a human would do if not limited by gravity, reality, and a lack of imagination. The Disney approach, which came to fruition with *Snow White*, enabled audiences to see not just these sorts of actions but also emotions, feelings, attitudes, and motivations communicated on the screen.

The early production notes for *Snow White* have been a gift to historians and animators because they show the process by which this fairy tale came to the screen. Walt started thinking about *Snow White* sometime in 1934, although it is possible he thought about it way before that: a silent version of *Snow White* with actors, not animation, was the first movie he remembers seeing in a theatre.[12] Some notes from late 1934 show that the characters and form of the story, which was borrowed from a 19th century fairy tale by the Grimm brothers, were nearly set, although it would be endlessly tweaked and edited in the years before release. Artists who worked on *Snow White* remember a multihour session with Walt in which he acted out every scene of the movie, doing every character and every voice and also explaining the emotions, motivations, and themes of the different sections. Walt's living storyboard for *Snow White* became the guiding structure through the years of production, but new ideas and gags were also solicited from the animators.

The character of Snow White was described in some early production notes as a "Janet Gaynor type," Gaynor being the silent-film actress who won the Academy Award for best actress in 1928. Douglas Fairbanks, once the model for Mickey Mouse cartoons, was back as the model for the type of prince the movie needed, only now about 18 years old. There were dozens of names for the seven dwarfs, the ones that finally made it into the movie—Happy, Grumpy, Sleepy, Doc, Bashful, Dopey, and Sneezy—and the ones that didn't—Jumpy, Scrappy, Crabby, Hotsy, Dippy, Gloomy, Nifty, Shifty, Thrifty, Dumpy, Doleful, Puffy, Snappy, Snoopy, Dirty, and Dizzy among others.[13]

All the details of the story, the music, the characters, the action, the voices, and the drawings were very carefully controlled with Walt intimately familiar with every step of the process. One technological problem had to be solved because the commitment made to a more realistic look demanded a better sense of perspective in the film. The Disney studio developed a multiplane camera, a setup in which five layers of glass plates, on which scenes and characters were painted, would be placed some distance apart under the camera. Because backgrounds should move less than foregrounds when the camera moves across a scene, or the foreground should get bigger more rapidly when the camera moved into the scene, the background and foreground needed to be separated. Previously, the action cels were just placed directly on the backgrounds but now the separation between them enabled both better action and more perspective. The studio applied for a patent on the camera (others, including Ub Iwerks in his studio, had also worked on such a camera), and Walt was granted the patent in 1940. *Snow White* was advertised as being in "Multiplane Technicolor." The camera was tested out in a *Silly Symphony* cartoon, *The Old Mill*, in 1937.

Everyone underestimated how much *Snow White* would cost—Walt and Roy had budgeted 500,000 dollars but it cost closer to 1.5 million dollars—and also how much work it would take to create: three years and at least 250,000 drawings (some reports say two million), with the staff now several hundred, including 75 animators. Walt was not always pleased with the work, but their deadlines and budget did not permit endless reworking of the flaws. He did, however, give bonuses or salary increases to some of the animators as incentives. He and Roy also had to deal with a new problem: figuring out how to distribute a feature instead of a short. Charlie Chaplin stepped in to help out, advising the Disneys on rates and strategies.[14] In a trailer produced to advertise the film, Walt was promoted as much as the story, and one screen stated, "See for yourself what the genius of Walt Disney has created in his first full length feature production."[15]

Snow White and the Seven Dwarfs premiered in December 1937, in Hollywood with dozens of famous stars showing up for the opening, including Douglas Fairbanks, Jr., Marlene Dietrich, Shirley Temple, Clark Gable, Carole Lombard, Norma Shearer, and Mickey and Minnie Mouse, Donald Duck, and the Seven Dwarfs. "Blasé Hollywood, accustomed to gala openings, turns out for the most spectacular of them all," explained a newsreel that advertised the film.[16] It was an immediate success, both with audiences (who jammed the theatres and waited in line to get in) and with critics (some called it one of the best films of the year), although a few critics dismissed the entire idea of an animated feature. *Variety* raved, "So perfect is the illusion, so tender the romance and fantasy, so emotional are certain portions when the acting of the characters strikes a depth comparable to the sincerity of human players, that the film approaches real greatness."[17] *Time* magazine's critic exclaimed, "Skeptical Hollywood, that had wondered whether a fairy story could have enough suspense to hold an audience through seven reels, and whether, even if the plot held up, an audience would care about the fate of characters who were just drawings, was convinced that Walt Disney had done it again."[18] Walt was featured on the cover with small statues of the seven dwarfs.[19]

The movie opened in New York at Radio City Music Hall in January 1938 and played for four months. The *New York Times* reviewer explained what this unprecedented film was like: "You can visualize it best if you imagine a child, with a wondrous, Puckish imagination, nodding over his favorite fairy tale and dreaming a dream in which his story would come true ... But no child, of course, could dream a dream like this. For Mr. Disney's humor has the simplicity of extreme sophistication." This is exactly what Walt hoped to accomplish, making dreams come true, and making a film that appealed to adults as much as to children.

Throughout 1938 *Snow White* was not only in theatres across America but also all over the world in 10 foreign language editions and 49 countries. *Snow White and the Seven Dwarfs* was a huge hit, bringing in around 8 million dollars at the box office (when tickets were less than a quarter for adults, a dime for kids; this would be several hundred million dollars translated into today's dollars). It became the box office champion, bringing in more money than any other movie up to that time. After its initial run in 1937–38, it was withdrawn from the theatres, only to be reintroduced years later, eight times in all, the first time in 1944. This began the Disney practice of putting films "in the vault" and holding off the market for a specified period. The songs from the movie, "Some Day My Prince Will Come," "Whistle While You Work," and "Heigh-Ho," became musical standards, widely known and regularly recorded and performed.

The film earned Walt another special Academy Award which stated that *Snow White and the Seven Dwarfs* was "recognized as a significant screen innovation which has charmed millions and pioneered a great new entertainment field for the motion picture cartoon." The award consisted of one large Oscar and seven little ones. As with Mickey Mouse, *Snow White and the Seven Dwarfs* appeared as many different products: 147 different companies were reported to have produced over

2,000 different types of merchandise. Books of the story sold 20 million copies while dolls and figurines sold 2 million and drinking glasses sold more than 16 million.[20]

Snow White is considered the first film in what has been called the Golden Age of Disney animation. Between the release of *Snow White* and World War II, Walt produced his best and most famous feature animations: *Pinocchio* (1940), *Fantasia* (1940), *Dumbo* (1941), and *Bambi* (1942).

NOTES

1. Miller, Diane Disney, and Pete Martin. "When the Animals Began to Talk." *Saturday Evening Post*, December 8, 1956, p. 85.

2. Ibid.

3. Thomas, Bob. *Walt Disney: An American Original*. New York: Hyperion, 1994, p. 120.

4. Schindehette, Susan. "Growing Up Disney." *People*, December 21, 1998. Available at http://www.people.com/people/archive/article/0,20127119,00.html. Accessed April 11, 2010.

5. Barrier, Michael. *The Animated Man: A Life of Walt Disney*. Berkeley: University of California Press, 2007, p. 94.

6. Watts, Steven. *The Magic Kingdom: Walt Disney and the American Way of Life*. Boston: Houghton Mifflin, 1997, pp. 79–81.

7. Quoted in Blechman, R. O. "The Art of Walt Disney." *New York Times*, December 2, 1973, p. 55.

8. Disney, Walt. Walt Disney Productions Inter office Communication, December 23, 1935. Available at: http://www.animationmeat.com/pdf/nineoldmen/MemoFromWalt.pdf. Accessed April 11, 2010.

9. Ibid.

10. Thomas, p. 124.

11. Thomas, Frank, and Ollie Johnston. *The Illusion of Life: Disney Animation*. New York: Hyperion, 1995, p. 11.

12. Finch, Christopher. *The Art of Walt Disney: From Mickey Mouse to the Magic Kingdoms*. Rev. and expanded. New York: H. N. Abrams, 2004, p. 123.

13. Ibid., pp. 123–25.

14. Gabler, Neal. *Walt Disney: The Triumph of the American Imagination*. New York: Knopf, 2006, pp. 266–71.

15. Trailer available at http://www.youtube.com/watch?v=5kWr9e4JN5I. Accessed April 11, 2010.

16. RKO-Pathe. "Fantasy Filmland Thrills To 'Snow White.'" 1937.

17. Flinn, John C., Sr. "Snow White and the Seven Dwarfs." *Variety*, December 29, 1937.

18. "Cinema: Mouse and Man." *Time*, December 27, 1937.

19. The cover can be viewed at: http://www.time.com/time/covers/0,16641,19371227,00.html. Accessed April 11, 2010.

20. Pryor, Thomas M. "'Snow White' Sidelights; Censors Toppled and Business Boomed as the Dwarfs Went Round the World." *New York Times*, February 5, 1939.

Chapter 7

THE END OF AN ERA

As 1937 changed into 1938, Walt entered one of his most complex years. The studio was already working on other projects when *Snow White and the Seven Dwarfs* was released. Walt was collaborating with conductor Leopold Stokowski on recording the score for an elaborate animation sequence called "The Sorcerer's Apprentice" that eventually was used in *Fantasia*, which was like a feature-length *Silly Symphony*. Preliminary work on *Pinocchio* and *Bambi* were under way. Walt and Roy purchased land in Burbank for a new studio, one that would be the ideal workspace and have state-of-the-art equipment for his staff. By the beginning of 1940, all the departments were enjoying the large campus, built at the cost of at least three million dollars, that still is used by Disney today. The new studio, designed mostly by Walt, had a very thoughtful design based on years of experience with animators and their working conditions.

In June, Walt was awarded three honorary master's degrees from several prestigious universities. The University of Southern California was first, honoring him for "bringing to youngsters the spirit of innocent childhood, and bringing to oldsters a bit of their second childhood."[1] For the Yale degree, he was honored because he was said to have been a "creator of a new language of art, who has brought the joy of deep laugh-ter to millions and, by touching the heart of humanity without distinc-tion of race, has served as ambassador of international good-will" and "accomplished something that defied all the efforts and experiments of the laboratories in zoology and biology; he has given impressive signifi-cance to the word anima in animated; he has given animals souls."[2]

At Harvard he was under consideration for a degree along with Jo-seph P. Kennedy, Sr., who at the time was ambassador to the United Kingdom as well as a wealthy businessman who had a foothold in Hol-lywood. Kennedy helped organize several studios and their vaudeville theatres in the 1920s into RKO, which later distributed some Disney films. Kennedy was not chosen for the award (at the college several of his soon-to-be-famous sons attended) but Walt was. At the ceremony, Walt was described as a "magician who has created a modern dwelling for the muses."[3] These honorary degrees were just 3 of the nearly 900 awards Walt and the studio would earn in his lifetime, including 48 Oscars and 7 Emmys.

The triumph of Snow White, the expansion of the studio, and the recognition Walt was receiving for his work were offset for the Disneys by a horrible tragedy. Roy and Walt's parents, Elias and Flora, were living in Portland, Oregon, up to this point because their son Herb and daughter Ruth were there. But for years they had been wanting to move to California to be near their two successful sons, Walt and Roy. Elias and Flora still supported themselves but were getting older, and Herb moved away while Ruth married a somewhat unreliable man. At the urging of Roy and Walt, Flora and Elias moved to California early in 1938 and later in the year moved into a house that Walt and Roy built just for them, close to Roy's house. The house had a furnace that was built incorrectly and it leaked carbon monoxide into the living quarters. One day in November, both Flora and Elias were overcome by the gas; Flora died and while Elias recovered, he was different after that until his death in 1941.

Feature animation projects were already lined up, and the studio con-tinued to create short cartoons to help pay the bills even as Walt and Roy were experiencing this family tragedy. The Silly Symphony series ended in 1939, with the last one, the color remake of The Ugly Duck-ling, winning an Oscar for Best Cartoon. But several of the innovative

*Donald Duck, Minnie and Mickey Mouse, and two
of the Seven Dwarfs pose with their creator, Hollywood producer Walt Disney, after he received an
honorary Master of Arts degree at commencement at
Harvard University, Cambridge, Massachusetts, on
June 23, 1938. (AP Photo)*

feature animations from this period did not perform well financially.
The next feature released after *Snow White* was *Pinocchio* in February
1940. *Pinocchio*, the story of a wooden puppet that wants to be a boy,
was not as successful at the box office as hoped despite the even more
dramatic improvements in animation it demonstrated. It cost 2.6 million dollars to make, and this amount was difficult to earn back, not
only because the depression continued but also because the overseas
markets were closed as war began in Europe in 1939. Next came *Fantasia*, which was released as a special long-run feature in theatres with
a special sound system in November 1940. The setup made it difficult
to make a profit as did the unusual nature of the film, which combined
classical music with unusual animation in a nonlinear and sometimes

surreal style. The feature-length movie actually started as a short film featuring the sequence with Mickey Mouse, *The Sorcerer's Apprentice*. It was expanded, however, because the shorts did not earn enough to cover the costs. *Fantasia* was considered a box office and critical loser for years, although later releases of it proved very successful.

In April 1940, the Disneys offered stock in the studio as a way to pay off its loans. The stock was popular and sold easily (some was given to employees), but there was still not enough money to continue the production schedule, so more loans were in order and the studio continued to be in debt. Production on *Dumbo* continued into 1941, and it was released to good reviews and a strong box office in October 1941. The *New York Times* described it as, "the most genial, the most endearing, the most completely precious cartoon feature film ever to emerge from the magical brushes of Walt Disney's wonder-working artists!"[4] The studio also released an unusual film in June 1941 called *The Reluctant Dragon*. It was a combination animation and behind-the-scenes look at the way the studio operated. It was also a fore-shadowing of the types of stories Walt would do with his television programs a decade later.

Dumbo became another cultural reference point, like Mickey Mouse and like Walt himself. Dozens of other movies over the years have made reference to the flying elephant. Even today, animal activities point to the unpleasant conditions in many American zoos, especially for elephants, and cite the Dumbo factor: "Free Dumbo! Zoos are Bad for Elephants," states one such article.[5] In the years of the world war that came soon after Dumbo's release, the plucky elephant was also a reference. One B-17 bomber in the Pacific called itself Dumbo and painted a picture of Disney's elephant on the side. More generally, Dumbos and Superdumbos were terms applied to large military planes. The movie also contains a reference to the strike that took place while it was being made and shows a bunch of clowns in the circus trying to hit the boss up for a raise.

After *Snow White*, the work routine and the atmosphere at the studio seemed to change. Descriptions of Walt's work habits vary widely either because people remember different aspects of him or he acted differently with different types of people, or because the desired story of Walt is served by one memory or another. In any case, some people described Walt at this time as indirect with his praise but showing appreciation by rewarding bonuses, and they remember him as being open to suggestions but always wanting to carry out his vision.[6] Others remember a Walt who "responded gracelessly to the pressures" of his life, treating his employees harshly and critically.[7]

Walt's darker mood has been attributed to the need to cash in on *Snow White*'s success quickly and avoid layoffs, so the approach to animating the new project, *Pinocchio*, seemed to have changed: now Walt held story sessions in which he "barked" at his staff and constantly requested rewrites on the script.[8] Some people remember Walt calling his animators "my boys" in a negative, paternalistic way; others saw it as a desire to keep the sense of the animators as his happy family.[9] Walt, however, continued to call his studio staff "my boys" well into the 1960s. If nothing else, the increased size of the studio made it impossible for Walt to know everyone as he had done in the early days, and his personal charisma, so important for getting projects through in the past, was not reaching all the workers.

In the new facility as in the old, there was a hierarchy that developed among the staff. This was not unique to the Disney studio, and the division of labor that became so newly evident in the Disney studio was an established part of production facilities across Hollywood. At the top of the hierarchy were the best animators, the Nine Old Men. These were the guys (and they were all men in the Disney shop) who had access to the best offices, assistants, a private lounge, food deliveries to their offices, and extra compensation. These were the key animators on *Snow White* and the other feature projects, called the Nine Old Men by Walt apparently as a take on a comment that President Roosevelt had made about the aging members of his Supreme Court. While they were not quite as old or controversial as the sitting justices, the Nine Old Men set a standard for animation that still affects productions today, so their legendary status was well-deserved even if it highlighted the inequalities of the system. Yet even these artists did not get screen credit for their work; only Walt usually did, and this was likely one of the inequalities that seemed to have been a factor in the decision of about one third of the staff to go on strike.

In a book on animation techniques that were developed in the Disney studio, two of the Nine Old Men (Frank Thomas and Ollie

Johnston) wrote that Walt should be recognized for promoting all the major innovations they described. While others were decrying the system Walt set up, Thomas and Johnston credited Walt with making their innovative work possible because of the work flow that he set up, the training he provided, and because of his "insistence and supervision."[10] The loose, rough sketches Walt encouraged and the assistants he provided freed up his Nine Old Men to innovate and experiment. Walt, Thomas and Johnston explained,

> never did build an organization in the strictest sense of that word. What he built was a loosely unified group of talented people with particular abilities who could work together in continually changing patterns. They did this with a minimum of command and a maximum of dedication. What Walt wanted was the greatest creative effort—not the most efficient operation. ... This method worked because Walt was the boss—not just because it was his studio or that he had the authority to get what he wanted, but because his ideas were the best.[11]

Many years later, a young fan was trying to understand how this group production worked and just what, in a sense, Walt's work as a supervisor was. In 1956, Walt recounted this exchange (as retold by his daughter):

> "Mr. Disney, do you draw all those pictures yourself?"
> "No," Dad said.
> "You do the first ones, don't you?" the boy asked.
> "At one time I drew them all," Dad told him; "then, later, I did the first ones and had the others done by other artists, but today I draw none of them."
> The boy refused to give up, "But you think up all the ideas, don't you, Mr. Disney?"
> "No," Dad said, "I have men who work on ideas and I work with them; then we all team up to make it come out right."
> The boy looked disgusted. "What do you do, Mr. Disney?" he asked, "That," said Dad, "is a good question."[12]

What was especially clear at the studio was the inconsistency in the compensation and responsibilities attached to any particular job. Walt's manner of awarding bonuses and salaries has been described as based on his "personal discretion and memory" and has been called arbitrary, inconsistent, and subjective.[13] Unequal bonuses after successful movie release and unequal distributions of stock options when the company went public in 1940 are also often cited as problematic. When the Disney studio was later engaged in negotiations to settle the strike that hit it in 1941, it was ordered by the U.S. Labor Department to correct its policies by making available "official job classifications and equalization of salaries, regular grievance procedures, paid vacations, severance pay, minimum guarantees of employment."[14]

This approach to the studio's animation projects was about to be tested with the addition of new staff (staff totaled at least 1,000 in the early 1940s), a move into a new facility, more feature animation work, an approaching war, a downturn in the overseas markets, and a questioning of the way the studio was run that resulted in the devastating 1941 strike. There were still budget woes because, as usual, Roy and Walt put the money they earned from *Snow White* back into the business, after they paid off the loans they took out to make it. Roy also found it difficult to fire anyone, especially in the depression, and the staff got too large for the work that was available. While Roy was asking for salary cuts, apparently Walt was secretly giving salary raises.[15] In 1940, Ub Iwerks returned and because he had stopped actually doing animation, he was eventually given the job of director of technical research, which he held for the next 30 years. He was a key factor in the special effects advances made by the studio over the years as well as in developing the theme park attractions and rides. He won two Academy Awards for his work.

Across the country at this time, great changes were under way. It was a "political and cultural realignment" that shifted the center of cultural change from the East Coast to Hollywood and injected politics into popular forms of entertainment, especially the movies.[16] This was true not only of the content of the movies of the time but also the developing relationship between the studio heads and their workers. The conflict between the creative people who wrote and created the movies, and the business people who financed and distributed them, was increasing. In many cases the studio heads were "autocratic" in their management techniques.[17]

The 1930s also saw many more workers seeking unionization as a way to protect their jobs so that by 1940 about 27 percent of all workers across the country were unionized.[18] Work stoppages or strikes were also increasing. The period from the late 1930s to 1941 has also been called the second Red Scare because it is during this time that Congress began investigating so-called un-American activities, especially by perceived communists. In 1938, Congressman Martin Dies, Jr., a Democrat from Texas, announced plans to investigate Hollywood and its infiltration by communists, including those who were accused of taking over the Hollywood trade unions. The Screen Writers Guild (SWG), formed by writers in opposition to the industry-run Screen Playwrights, was accused of communist infiltration when it gained negotiating power in 1939. When the Soviet Union signed a nonaggression pact with Nazi Germany, also in 1939, communists became identified with the other undesirable movements of the time, Nazism and fascism, and anticommunism strengthened. Some Hollywood studio executives told their workers that communist activities would not be tolerated.[19] Claims that communists were involved in the trade unions of Hollywood was the connection that helped explain to Walt why his workers went on strike. It also shows that the Disney studio situation was not unique and that Walt's approach had parallels across Hollywood.

Several of the major animation studios (including the Fleischer Studios, MGM, and Warner Bros.) had already been unionized by the Screen Cartoonists Guild (SCG) with a seasoned union organizer, Herbert Sorrell, leading the unionization drive. Disney, the most famous studio, was to be next. Walt had organized an in-house union called the Federation of Screen Cartoonists (FSC) that he thought should represent his workers. Its negotiating powers were limited to asking for higher wages and better working conditions but not to going on strike.[20] Walt wanted a secret ballot so that workers could choose between SCG and FSC, but the representatives of SCG claimed to already have the majority of votes from the workers. The National Labor Relations Board, set up by Congress in 1935 to administer the laws governing the relationship between unions, workers, and employers, received a complaint from the SCG about Disney in early 1941.

At the same time, the animators were beginning to meet, both inside and outside the studio, to talk about their work situation.[21] One of the most active organizers was an animator who worked at the studio since 1932, Arthur Babbitt. Babbitt and Walt were often at odds and when Babbitt started union organizing activities, including becoming the in-house representative of the SCG, the studio attempted to discredit him, both in terms of the union work and his animation.

Walt sent an interoffice communication to his employees in February 1941 warning them not to spend company time on union activities. He also called a meeting of his staff in the same month and read a statement about the situation. He explained his unwavering passion for animation and his fear that if the Disney studio ended, cartoons would be crass and based simply on economics. His explanation for the disparities in the status of the various workers was a harsh statement of survival of the fittest: "It's the law of the universe that the strong shall survive and the weak must fall by the way." Walt later testified before Congress that it was Herbert Sorrell, and not any actual conditions in the studio, that caused the strike. Negotiations continued into May 1941.

When the Disney studio laid off 24 of the activist workers who were SCG members, including Arthur Babbitt, a strike was called in May 1941. Striking animators and staff picketed in front of the new Burbank facility, carrying creative signs that read "Are We Mice or Men?" and with a picture of Pinocchio, "There are no strings on me." Jiminy Cricket from the same movie was on a sign that said "Taint Cricket to pass a picket!" One sign read "We made Fantasia" and another "Snow White and the 700 Dwarfs." A sign saying "I'd rather be a dog than a scab" featured Mickey's dog, Pluto, as did one that stated "I have a bone to pick with Walt." The strikers set up a tent camp across the street from the studio and were supported by union workers at nearby Lockheed and Warner Bros.

As the strike continued into the summer, other creative actions included marchers dressed as hooded, bare-chested executioners carrying a guillotine with a sign that read "Happy Birthday to Gunther and Walt." A large-scale dragon carried by eight men had the word "unfair" painted on its body and featured Walt's head and a sign around its neck that said "The Reluctant Disney." Picketers in New York at showings of *The Reluctant Dragon* wore Mickey, Donald, and the Seven Dwarfs masks. The number of striking workers was hard to determine but was several hundred by all estimates, up to half the entire staff. Two head animators, Art Babbitt and Bill Tytla, joined the picket lines and production inside the studio could barely continue. The greatest loss for the studio may have been the creative work atmosphere: as one animator commented, "The esprit de corps that made possible all the brilliant films of the 1930s was as dead as a dodo."[22]

Some consumer groups joined in boycotting Disney films and products. A group called the Hollywood League of Women Shoppers sent Walt a letter saying they were siding with the workers and would advise their members, who were interested in the work conditions of employees, that Disney was unfair to its workers. Walt was later to cite their actions when he was being questioned about the communist influence in Hollywood at the HUAC hearings in 1947. Boycotts of Walt and his crew when they were in South America were also threatened though it is difficult to know if they were carried out.

In a letter written by the strikers to communicate their side of the events and the failed negotiations, the animators said they were striking for "the future security of all Disney employees and the future health of the business."[23] They objected to the introduction of reputed mobster Willie Bioff into the negotiations and reminded their fellow strikers that they did not believe that Walt was a "cheap, chiseling hypocrite" as he was called by one of the Screen Actors Guild's negotiators. Instead they saw Walt as someone whose "sole interest is making movies" and not altruistically caring for his workers.[24]

Walt and Roy were being advised in their negotiations by Gunther Lessing, their lawyer. He recommended a hard line against the strikers. Many later accused Lessing of inciting Walt to believe that communists had been responsible for the strike. A full page ad addressed to the workers from Walt was published in two industry newspapers in July. In the ad Walt states, "I believe that you have been misled and misinformed about the real issues underlying the strike at the studio. I am positively convinced that Communistic agitation, leadership, and activities have brought about this strike."[25] Soon after this personal message to his striking staff, the studio fired many of the striking workers and the studio was shut down for several weeks.

Walt was to carry this opinion about communist influences on his staff for many years, along with his personal offense at his family of animators turning on him and being ungrateful for the work and experience he was giving them. To Walt, the strikers were the problem, not him. He explained some years later about the strike:

> It was probably the best thing that ever happened to me, for it eventually cleaned house at our studio a lot more thoroughly than I could have done. I didn't have to fire anybody to get rid of the chip-on-the-shoulder boys and the world-owes-me-a-living lads. An elimination process took place I couldn't have forced if I'd wanted to. Our organization sifted down to the steady, dependable people. The others have gone.[26]

The strike wasn't resolved until September when Walt was away on a goodwill trip to South America. He was encouraged to get away from the situation after the strike was in its fifth week, and he saw it as a chance to do this after being convinced by Roy and Gunther Lessing. World War II was spreading quickly and the U.S. government was concerned that its neighbors to the south would side with the forces of fascism in Europe. Nelson Rockefeller was in charge of the Office of the Coordinator of Inter-American Affairs (CIAA), an agency tasked with providing news, advertising, movies, and radio to Latin America, especially as a way of eliminating the German influence there. It utilized blacklists of media outlets it considered incompatible with the goals of the free world and disseminated propaganda highlighting cooperation between the Americas. Gunther Lessing was also associated with the office.

The trip, taking Walt, his wife Lilly, and 18 crew members, would show off one of America's favorite patriots and give Walt a chance to make some of the films the government wanted to use to persuade Brazil, Chile, Argentina, and Peru to avoid Nazism and favor the Allies. The incentive for Walt was a contract for four films and a healthy budget of 270,000 dollars as well as a new market. Since the war had started in 1939, the European markets were unavailable for the distribution of his films, and foreign film revenues had accounted for about 45 percent of the studio's income. Encouraged by the government that the strike would be taken care of, Walt and his team left for what he considered a working trip to gather material for several motion pictures.

Walt produced an animated/live-action feature film with four different segments based in South America called *Saludos Amigos*. The film, released in Brazil in 1942 and the United States in 1943, earned over a million dollars for the studio and served the government's purpose of promoting solidarity in the Western Hemisphere. Walt's work in South America came under scrutiny in later decades as academics became concerned about the imperialist tendencies of multinational companies to replace indigenous cultures with their homogenized ones.[27]

During the trip, the strike was settled with the new union, SCG, getting control of representing the workers. The settlement resulted in pay raises and better working conditions for all workers and the institution of coherent pay and responsibility guidelines. The days of the one great big, happy, creative family were over. During the trip, Elias Disney, Walt's father, died.

NOTES

1. Barrier, Michael. "A Day in the Life: Disney, June 23, 1938." Available at http://www.michaelbarrier.com/Essays/WaltAtHarvard/WaltAtHarvard.html. Accessed April 11, 2010.

2. Ibid.

3. Watts, Steven. *The Magic Kingdom: Walt Disney and the American Way of Life*. Boston: Houghton Mifflin, 1997, p. 124.

4. Crowther, Bosley. "Walt Disney's Cartoon, 'Dumbo,' a Fanciful Delight, Opens at the Broadway." *New York Times*, October 24, 1941.

5. Kluger, Jeffrey. "Free Dumbo! Zoos Are Bad for Elephants," *Time*, December 11, 2008.

6. Thomas, Bob. *Walt Disney: An American Original*. New York: Hyperion, 1994, p. 188.

7. Schickel, Richard. *The Disney Version: The Life, Times, Art, and Commerce of Walt Disney*. 3rd ed. Chicago: Ivan R. Dee, 1997, p. 250.

8. Gabler, Neal. *Walt Disney: The Triumph of the American Imagination*. New York: Knopf, 2006, pp. 292–93.

9. Ibid., p. 354.

10. Thomas, Frank, and Ollie Johnston. *The Illusion of Life: Disney Animation*. New York: Hyperion, 1995, p. 38.

11. Ibid., p. 185.

12. Miller, Diane Disney, and Pete Martin. "My Dad, Walt Disney." *Saturday Evening Post*, November 17, 1956, p. 134.

13. Nohria, Nitin, Anthony J. Mayo, and Bridget Gurtler. "Walt Disney and the 1941 Animators' Strike." *Harvard Business School Case Studies* (2008), p. 7.

14. Ibid., p. 9.

15. Gabler, pp. 349–50.

16. Langdon, Jennifer E. *Caught in the Crossfire: Adrian Scott and the Politics of Americanism in 1940s Hollywood*. New York: Columbia University Press, 2008, p. 18. Available at http://www.gutenberg-e.org/langdon/. Accessed April 11, 2010.

17. Ibid.

18. Nohria, Mayo, and Gurtler, p. 16.

19. Ceplair, Larry. "The Film Industry's Battle against Left-Wing Influences, from the Russian Revolution to the Blacklist." *Film History*. Vol. 20, 2008, p. 405.

20. Nohria, Mayo, and Gurtler, p. 8.

21. Gabler, p. 357.

22. Denning, Michael. *The Cultural Front: The Laboring of American Culture in the Twentieth Century*. Brooklyn, NY: Verso, 1998, p. 413.

23. Animators' letter available at http://matterhorn1959.blogspot.com/2008_04_01_archive.html. Accessed April 11, 2010.

24. Ibid.

25. Nohria, Mayo, and Gurtler, p. 10.

26. Miller, Diane Disney, and Pete Martin. "Mickey Mouse Becomes a Secret Weapon." *Saturday Evening Post*, December 29, 1956, p. 74.

27. See Dorfman, Ariel, and Armand Mattelart. *How to Read Donald Duck: Imperialist Ideology in the Disney Comic*. Translated by David Kunzle. New York: International General, 1971.

Chapter 8

WORLD WAR II PROPAGANDA

When Walt returned from his trip to South America, he found the strike settled and, as Roy put it in a letter to prepare him, things were different at the studio. With a reduced staff and a chilled atmosphere, production on Walt's beloved features was difficult to get started again. Work was underway on the South American package of four short animations with live-action footage between segments called *Saludos Amigos*, which was eventually released in August 1942. The second Latin American project, *The Three Caballeros*, was one of the few nongovernmental projects during this period, and it showed an advanced use of live actors combined with animation, much like Walt had attempted 20 years earlier with the *Alice* movies.

The strike by the Disney studio staff in the summer of 1941 marked the end of what is commonly called the Golden Age of Disney feature animations. With the release of *Dumbo* in the summer of 1941 and *Bambi* in 1942, the animated feature production of original fictional stories was almost idle until the end of the war. The strike had resulted in the layoff of several hundred workers when production came to a halt, and now some but not all of them were now back. Later, animator and strike leader Art Babbitt was given notice, along with 200 other people, when the studio needed to lay off more workers after the arbitration agreement. A Western Union telegram to one of the striking animators from Gunther Lessing unceremoniously said, "It is necessary to reduce our staff and we are sorry we have to extend your present layoff indefinitely."[1] Babbitt contested the layoff and was able to get his job back after serving in the war.

Many of the artists and animators in the studio were draft age, and many were called for duty as the war developed. After the American

Walt Disney, creator of Mickey Mouse, poses at the Pancoast Hotel in Miami, Florida, on August 13, 1941. An animation innovator, Disney featured his favorite character in Steamboat Willie, *the first short cartoon with a soundtrack, in September 1928. He released his first full-length animated film,* Snow White and the Seven Dwarfs, *in 1937. A multimedia visionary whose name became synonymous with family entertainment, Disney expanded into television and book publishing, and led the way for a new kind of amusement park known as the "theme park." Disney opened Disneyland in California in 1955. (AP/Wide World Photos)*

entry into the war, Walt tried to convince the military that his staff could serve as well by staying in the studio and making the war films, and this worked to retain some of the men. Sometimes men were drafted and then assigned to the studio to work on government projects, but most often the men went overseas. Some of the striking animators moved on to other studios or set up their own operations and ended up creating new animation styles and some of the most successful cartoon characters of the last half of the 20th century. The "Civil War of Animation" left its mark on the industry and on Walt Disney for years to come.[2]

On Sunday, December 7, 1941, at 7:48 AM Hawaiian time, the Japanese attacked Pearl Harbor and the United Stated entered World War II. Thirty-five hundred Americans were killed or wounded, and the United States had to declare war on Japan and Italy, and Germany declared war on the United States in turn. The beginning of the war marked a new era for the studio and Walt. Immediately after the attack, Walt got a phone call telling him that the U.S. Army was moving 700 soldiers into the Disney studio, which they used as a base for protecting the local aircraft factories, especially Lockheed. The Army moved its antiaircraft operation there and they took over much of the studio. The soldiers stayed for eight months but the studio wasn't paid for the use of the space for a few years. The militarization of the studio meant that workers had to wear identification and be cleared by military security guards. The additional scrutiny did not help the atmosphere and even more artists left the studio. A bit of regular cartoon animation continued, but Walt was tapped by the government for a different kind of work. He was asked to begin producing instructional and public relations films for the military and the federal government.

The military asked Walt to produce a wide array of instructional and educational films. The studio was not completely new to doing such films. Back in 1922, Walt had, of course, made one of his first instructional films for a dentist, *Tommy Tucker's Tooth*. But he had also done a film on speculation for the Lockheed Corporation, the airline manufacturer and defense contractor which was located near his studio. The film, about riveting, was later sold to the Canadian government, which also commissioned other films as early as May 1941. One of the movies was for the National Film Board of Canada to support the sales of war bonds. Walt used the Big Bad Wolf and the Three Little Pigs for the animation and posters, with the wolf as a Nazi in the story *Thrifty*

Pig, which was released in December 1941. Walt had also just returned from South America and was considering how to put together the footage shot there, which was supposed to be used for "making films for the development of better understanding between North and South America," a project he wanted to expand to the entire world once the war started. "The motion picture can be more helpful than any other force," Walt claimed, for uniting the world.[3]

Much effort was focused on movies as a way to disseminate information effectively and efficiently. Disney's own newsletter to its recruited personnel stated that it was simply a matter of resources that kept movies from being used more in education in the past. With the advent of the war, the government investment in educational films produced by Disney would prove to everyone that this was the future of education. This idea became important later when Walt entered the production of *True-Adventure* nature films after the war. Animation was especially valued because it could "make clear those things not visible to the eye, because of inaccessibility or rapidity of occurrence." Combining these films with textbooks (or in many cases, comic books drawn by Disney) was considered the ideal scenario.[4] With 16 million personnel mobilized over the course of the war, training materials for the military had to be easily understood (not all recruits were educated and many could not read or write), interesting, and consistent. Even though Walt often expressed frustration working with the military with everybody thinking they could be a film producer, the studio ended up producing at least 75 films specifically for military purposes.

Soon after Pearl Harbor, nearly 90 percent of the studio's activities were devoted to this contract work. Down to a little over 500 workers now, the studio was still considered the ideal source of these films (although other studios produced some too) because Disney animation and its trademark characters seemed guaranteed to keep the audience's attention or make dull subjects interesting. Disney did educational films on an amazing array of topics that covered military strategies and tactics, repair of equipment, medical and hygiene concerns, training for paratroopers and gunners, aviation safety, weather conditions, shooting down enemy aircraft, marching, cleaning rifles, and just about everything else the military needed to prepare the millions of troops for combat and support. Some of the films were short simple animations but some were extensive. There was a 26-part, 207-minute project called *Rules of the Nautical Road* from 1942 and a six-hour film on maintaining and repairing aircraft.[5] Some Disney personnel reportedly learned to fly so that they could produce such films accurately.

A series of psychological films designed to expose the follies of fascism and promote American patriotism were developed by Disney with suggestions from the government, and all were released in 1942 and 1943. One was called *Reason and Emotion,* and its ultimate message was that Nazis let emotion rule while the proper balance is to let reason have the upper hand and emotion take a back seat. But it also gives a picture of proper patriotic and gendered behavior. The movie starts with a basic statement: we each have the ability to think and this is called reason; we each have the ability to feel and this is called emotion. Reason and emotion always battle for mastery, so the stage is set for a discussion of which should rule our decisions. The story first takes place inside the head of the average American man and woman. In the man, emotion is a caveman in the back of a vehicle driven by a professorial man. If the caveman takes over, he tries to pick up a strange woman and gets slapped. If the cavewoman in the female's head takes over, she overeats and gets fat.

The current state of the world during war demanded more than ever that the conflict between reason and emotion be controlled. While this certainly applied to the Nazi emotionalism discussed in the next part of the short, it also referred to civilian behavior. Not only should people behave but they should not let their emotions get out of control when they hear or read news about the war. "Don't believe everything you hear ... and don't be stampeded by hearsay," Reason explains to Emotion in a man's brain. That, explains the narrator, is the method used by Hitler. The Nazi "Superman" lets Hitler-saluting Emotions take over and destroy Reason through fear. The movie ends with Reason piloting an airplane with patriotic music playing. The short, like the others in this psychological series, is not subtle and plays as straightforward cultural propaganda (as it was intended). The technique of showing what went on inside the human body or head has been used in many Disney shorts, especially those with Goofy, and it showed up later in several theme park attractions.

The animation short *Chicken Little* continued the style of direct behavioral instruction. The clucking hens in this story are like gossiping women, the "jitterbirds" are a dancing "featherbrained crowd," the geese and ducks are shown hanging out drinking, and even the educated elites are given a questioning look. Chicken Little is a good egg, but Foxy Loxy uses a book of psychology to get what he wants. The quotes from the book are out of Hitler's autobiography, *Mein Kampf*, and suggest going after the most stupid member, Chicken Little, to bring down the entire group. In the end, the whole panicked group is herded into an oven-like cave and eaten by the fox.

In *Education for Death*, a 10-minute animated short on how Nazi teachers "indoctrinate youth with the subhuman philosophy of Germany's Evil Trinity [Hitler, Goebbels, Goering]," the Disney animators were using satire, humor, and ethnic stereotypes for their message.[6] Titled in the credits as *The Story of One of "Hitler's Children" as Adapted from Education for Death: The Making of the Nazi* by author Gregor Ziemer, the film starts seriously with the question, what makes a Nazi? The Disney newsletter described the work as an "entertainment short" and during the war such dark subjects were common productions. In *Education for Death*, little Hans, a German youth, is indoctrinated to believe through a reworking of fairy tales that the evils of democracy will be vanquished by a knight in shining armor, Adolph Hitler. Hitler speaks German gibberish that the animators invented, and he tries to save Sleeping Beauty/Germany who is seen as an enormous fräulein with a Viking helmet. Ironically, Disney is using the same criticism that had been leveled at him for years about the rewriting and revisionist view of fairy tales.

The most notable of the entertainment/propaganda works is a short featuring Donald Duck called *Der Fuehrer's Face*. Released in January 1943, it won the Academy Award for best cartoon and was a box office hit. The story, which Walt says he thought up himself, has Donald Duck experiencing a nightmare in which he is living as a worker in Nazi Germany.[7] He incessantly salutes everything with a "Heil Hitler." Swastikas are everywhere, from the wallpaper to the bushes and clouds outside and the soldiers' backsides. Breakfast for the poor worker is a piece of hard bread cut with a saw, a coffee bean dipped in a cup of water, and a spray of bacon and eggs aroma accompanied by a look at *Mein Kampf*.

Donald works on an assembly line, screwing tops on artillery shells, that requires him to salute a Hitler portrait every few seconds. It employs many of the traditional Disney visual gags. When he gets a vacation from the fuehrer, Donald exercises in front of a poster of the Alps, and the exercise keeps twisting him into a swastika. Donald goes mad when he is required to work overtime, and a bizarre sequence follows with clever animation. Donald then appears in his bed in patriotic pajamas: fortunately, he had been dreaming and he hugs his miniature Statue of Liberty exclaiming, "Am I glad to be a citizen of the United States of America!" Walt's patriotism, which first expressed itself in World War I and came to be one of his defining characteristics in his later years, got strong representation through these psychological works.

The film was originally called *Donald Duck in Nutziland* (or *Nutzy Land*) but a song from the film, titled "Der Fuehrer's Face," was released before the film came out and when it was a hit, the film was reworked to take on the title of the song that played on the radio and in homes across the country. The song was recorded by parody artist "Spike" Jones (somewhat like "Weird Al" Yankovic today) in June 1942 and released on record in September, four months before the film came out. It became one of the most popular songs of the wartime, and when a New York radio announcer offered a free copy of it to anyone who bought a 50-dollar U.S. war bond, sales spiked. It sold sheet music and records by the thousands and set the stage for the Disney cartoon in January 1943.

The song was written by Disney composer Oliver G. Wallace, who started work as an organist at silent movies and vaudeville. At Disney he did work on *Dumbo* and some Mickey shorts before "Der Fuehrer's Face." The request for a song from Walt was vague and intimidating, and he recounted in it a Disney publication:

Walt encountered me in the hall and gave me a rush order: "Ollie, I want a serious song, but it's got to be funny." The further information that it was to be for a picture telling Donald Duck's adventures in Nazi land didn't help very much. "What do you mean?" I asked. "Suppose the Germans are singing it," Walt offered. "To them, it's serious. To us, it's funny."[8]

To get this effect, Wallace used a familiar German-type song called a *Schnitzelbank,* which is both a call-and-response song to teach children as well as a party and pub song with group participation. It often uses a chart that shows pictures of common objects, and the first object on the chart is a *Schnitzelbank,* a wooden carving bench. The first question asked is "Ist Das nicht ein Schnitzelbank?" (Is this not a schnitzelbank?). The response is "Ja das Ist eine Schnitzelbank," and so on for each object. The Nazis in the Donald Duck cartoon ask if they are not supermen and isn't Naziland good, in English. The Wallace song also uses the style of an oompah band with its heavy bass beat. In short, the use of stereotypical German music adds to the critique of Nazi Germany, not just Nazi ideology. Such anti-German sentiment was common during the war.

The Disney studio also produced comic book instruction manuals. One example is "Winter Draws On: Meet the Spandules."[9] It is a 28-page booklet created for the Air Force in 1943 to teach pilots about cold-weather flying. "Spandules" is the term used in the booklet to personify the dangers pilots can encounter in icy conditions and they credited Disney with the creation of the creatures who look like horn-helmeted Viking ghosts. Walt wanted to use these imaginary creatures from the world of fairies and leprechauns to explain other dangers to pilots as well as to keep the reader interested. They were like the gremlins used by RAF pilot and children's author Roald Dahl, who wrote about being a pilot and the mysterious things that can go wrong in his book *The Gremlins.*[10] Other projects were more mundane in their storyline but still used the distinctive Disney touch. One manual, presented in *Life* magazine in 1942, showed how to get an antitank rifle to work correctly with detailed drawings.[11]

Several offices of the federal government also asked for Walt's help in selling the war. One of the early films he was asked to make was for the Internal Revenue Service and the Secretary of the Treasury. They wanted to get people to pay their taxes and with millions of new taxpayers (people who went into the war industries, especially women) some instruction was necessary. Walt and his staff devised a story with Donald Duck as an anxious and reluctant taxpayer who gets converted to his patriotic duty (in *The New Spirit,* 1942 and *The Spirit of '43*). The films were distributed by a consortium of Hollywood studios called the

Animator Walt Disney, second from left, hands over his sketch of a Mickey Mouse gas mask to Major General William Porter, right, in Washington, D.C., January 8, 1942. Civilian defense and chemical warfare officers planned to produce the design intended to encourage children to use their mask readily for protection during World War II. The man at left is not identified. (AP Photo)

War Activities Committee of the Motion Pictures Industry. It made a deal with the Office of War Information and the Roosevelt administration to provide its resources to get government films into movie theatres, free. In exchange, the government agreed not to draft important actors or to make feature-length films. The government got 10 percent of the available screen time for its messages and contracted productions.[12]

When the Secretary of the Treasury complained that using Donald Duck in a tax film made it all silly, Walt countered that Donald, introduced in 1934, was a well-known character that people would willingly go see. Donald, in fact, had become more popular than Mickey Mouse in the intervening years. Walt also knew that his own Donald Duck cartoons would not earn any money while a free government movie was in theatres, and despite getting paid for the Treasury job, he lost money on his own cartoon rentals.[13] In fact, for all the government contracts he had, Walt's work with the military and the government did not make the studio rich. Since a corporate decision had been made not to reap a profit from any of the contract work, Walt and Roy just kept the studio going with the government contracts and the few shorts they produced each year.

Some of the work the studio did was uncompensated. The studio artists designed insignias for airplanes, tanks, and shoulder patches worn by the troops. The insignias featured characters designed by the artists and the work was given away free without copyright restrictions. Several thousand were designed at a substantial cost to the company. Many of the insignias are now collector's items.[14] Disney artists contributed work for all sorts of other war-related projects on the home front as well, including books of art sold to raise money for the war, Victory beer bottle designs, greeting cards, posters for gasoline rationing and blood drives, cartoons for scrap metal drives, and ads for victory gardens.

Battleships were both symbolic of the U.S. Navy's power and actual strategic components in the sea war, so the attack on Pearl Harbor and the U.S. Pacific fleet there was considered significant. Walt became convinced later in the war that air power rather than sea power was the key to winning the war, and he put his entire studio behind the idea. *Victory through Air Power* was a pet project of Walt's, one that he wanted the studio to produce despite the fact that it was both an unpopular idea militarily and a less than compelling topic for a motion picture. Based on a book by Major Alexander P. de Seversky, it made a compelling argument both for the military strategy and for the use of animations to demonstrate military concepts. Part of the reason Walt wanted to do this film is that he was interested in the history of aviation and had intended to do an animated history of flight going into the past and extending into the speculative future. This animation sequence was included in *Victory through Air Power* as were live-action sequences. It is said that when Winston Churchill and Franklin Roosevelt saw the film, they were convinced of the importance of air power for winning the war. The movie received an Academy Award nomination for best score but lost money for the studio.

In February 1944, the studio rereleased *Snow White and the Seven Dwarfs* because there was no other feature in production. The box office was good and helped keep the studio going now that military films were winding down. *The Three Caballeros*, the second Latin American film, was finished and released in February 1945. The war ended in Europe in May of the same year and in the Pacific in September. The studio had managed to survive the war despite shortages of supplies and labor and lost foreign markets. But the war had also shown the studio new directions including educational and training films. Walt sometimes talked about the war as an opportunity, saying that despite the frustrations of working with the government and its lack of understanding about humor and animation, they had survived. He is quoted as saying, "It's hard to say good things about a war, but this is a tremendous opportunity to show what our medium can do. Not many people get a chance like this to help both their country and themselves."[15]

NOTES

1. Viewed at the UPA Legacy Project. Available at http://web. me.com/bosustow/UPApix/History.html. Accessed April 11, 2010.

2. Sito, Tom. "The Disney Strike of 1941: How It Changed Animation & Comics." *Animation World Magazine*, July 19, 2005. Available at http://www.awn.com/articles/people/disney-strike-1941-how-it-changed-animation-comics. Accessed April 11, 2010.

3. Parker, Ralph, ed. *Dispatch from Disney's*. Vol. 1, No. 1. Burbank, Calif.: Walt Disney Productions, 1943, p. 2.

4. Ibid.

5. Solomon, Charles. "The Disney Studio at War." In *Animation—Art and Industry: A Reader*. Edited by Maureen Furniss: New Barnet, UK: John Libbey Publishing, 2009.

6. Parker, p. 2.

7. Miller, Diane Disney, and Pete Martin. "Mickey Mouse Becomes a Secret Weapon." *Saturday Evening Post*, December 29, 1956, p. 75.

8. Wallace, Oliver, as told to Ralph Parker. "How I Wrote 'Der Fuehrer's Face.'" *Dispatch from Disney's*. Ralph Parker, ed. Vol. 1, No. 1. Burbank, Calif.: Walt Disney Productions, 1943. Available at http:// disneybooks.blogspot.com/2007/04/this-just-in-from-jim-korkis-ive-been.html. Accessed April 11, 2009.

9. The entire booklet can be viewed at http://contentdm.unl.edu/cdm4/item_viewer.php?CISOROOT=/comics&CISOPTR=176&CISOBOX=1&REC=17. Accessed April 11, 2010.

10. Skylighters. "Who Were the Gremlins?" Available at http://www.skylighters.org/disney/index2.html. Accessed April 11, 2010.

11. "Walt Disney Goes to War." *Life*, August 31, 1942. Available at http://www.animationarchive.org/2006/12/story-walts-war.html. Accessed April 11, 2010.

12. Maslowski, Peter. *Armed with Cameras: The American Military Photographers of World War II*. New York: Free Press, 1998, p. 258.

13. Miller and Martin, p. 74.

14. Examples of the insignias can be found at http://toonsatwar.blogspot.com/ and at http://www.skylighters.org/disney/. Accessed April 11, 2010.

15. Lesjak, David. "When Disney Went to War." *World War II*, September 2005, p. 56.

Chapter 9

HUAC

Just about everything changed after the war. Male soldiers returning home were confronted with women who had been active in the workforce and didn't necessarily want to give that up. African American soldiers who fought in Europe and the Pacific came back to a country that was yet to recognize how they had been battlefield equals. The economy had long since recovered from the Great Depression and the country itself was now confirmed as one of the great world powers. The symbolic fallout of the atomic bomb, dropped on the cities of Nagasaki and Hiroshima in Japan, hung over world for the rest of the century, and the Cold War politics that resulted from the war and the bomb defined the nation for decades.

At the Disney studio, the war had not been as profitable as it had been on the other Hollywood lots. The decision by Disney's board to not profiteer from its work with the government meant that the studio inadvertently lost money on government projects. By war's end, a four million dollar debt weighed down the studio's postwar recovery. Walt's critics also saw the once innovative studio as outdated and stuck with its eyes looking to the past and not the future. Work commenced on the animation feature *Cinderella,* and its release in 1950 may have been an indication that Disney feature animations were back, but other developments in the Disney studio left critics wondering.

Nearly every biographer has insisted that Walt, by the time the war ended, was lost too, that his ambitions and creativity were drifting, that the passion to make innovative animations was gone. One suggested that "the guiding light of the Disney Studio had lost confidence in his ability, and maybe even his desire, to create the very special films for which he had become famous."[1] This was demonstrated vividly by the scathing reviews of the combination live-action/animated feature *Song of the South* that came out in late 1946. The movie was criticized both aesthetically and politically, its depiction of southern blacks in postwar America considered insensitive if not outright racist as the civil rights movement was gaining steam.[2]

Another biographer saw Walt in that early postwar period as "adrift" and even though he sought out collaborations with creative artists like Salvador Dali, the years between 1947 and 1949 were "lost" and attempts to reorganize the studio were hopeless because "the cult was over"[3] and the studio was experiencing "creative bankruptcy" with its attempts to simply compile old short animations into new bundled packages for quick box office success.[4] But a different perspective saw Walt's' scattered activities as an attempt to find a new direction that looked both back to the animations and the wartime work, and forward to new possibilities. According to Walt, "Now I need to diversify further, and that meant live action."[5] But before Walt could get his creative life back on track, he took a little detour.

First, back in 1941, right before the beginning of the U.S. involvement in World War II and right after the devastating animators' strike at his studio, Walt had joined with several other independent Hollywood producers to form the Society of Independent Motion Picture Producers (SIMPP). The people who formed the SIMPP, including Charlie Chaplin, Orson Welles, Samuel Goldwyn, and Mary Pickford, were reacting to the monopolies that the large studios had over distribution. This was especially problematic because the studios also owned the theatres where films were shown, and they often required block bookings, which meant that theatre managers had to buy multiple films, sight unseen, ahead of time in order to get the one film they wanted.

This practice of block bookings and blind bidding made it hard for independently produced films, like those of Disney, to get exhibited unless they worked out a distribution deal with one of the big studios. Their chief opposition on this issue was the Motion Picture Association of America (MPAA) which had been involved in censorship battles in the 1930s and '40s and formed the Hays Code then. The fight over block booking had been underway since the 1920s so this was not a new battle for either side, and the SIMPP led the way in a long-awaited federal battle. It did not end until 1948 when the Supreme Court ruled that the major studios had to get rid of their movie chains and stop block booking. The SIMPP included members of all political persuasions, with Chaplin and Welles being much more liberal than Disney and his conservative friends, but they still all worked together on this issue crucial to independent producers.

In October 1941, Jack Tenney, a state assemblyman in California and the head of the Assembly Fact Finding Committee on Un-American Activities in that state, began holding hearings that looked for communist influences in California politics. Walt Disney reportedly sent Tenney a letter telling him about Herbert Sorrell and his belief that the strike in his studio was communist inspired and Sorrell was the cause; Sorrell was called to testify at the Tenney hearings.[6] Tenney turned his attention more fully to Hollywood after this, and his hearings on the subject were similar to those being conducted on the federal level.

Communism is an ideology, a political party, and a worldview as well as a form of government. It's basic premise is that the problems of society are due to the unequal distribution of, and access to, wealth, and it is necessary for workers to right this wrong. In Hollywood, this correction to capitalism was seen as taking place through the formation of unions and through strikes. Communist propaganda was feared as a hidden element in the screenplays written by communist writers or in movies directed or produced by those who sympathized with communist ideas.

The search for communism in Hollywood was not totally misdirected because it was an ideology that had much appeal for some people. As one historian describes the situation:

The strength and appeal of the Party ... in the 1930s and 1940s was such that every progressive in America had to grapple at some point with the question: "Should I join?" Many chose not to. Some were put off by the hierarchical structure of the Party, others by the rigidity of some of the communists themselves. ... The Party's appeal to social idealism gave it a strong toehold among Hollywood progressives, and in fact, many Hollywood Communists have insisted that their experiences within the Party were markedly different from those of Communists in other industries or locales. From the beginning, the Party's desire to attract Hollywood luminaries translated into a relaxation of both discipline and dogma. Founded in 1934, the Hollywood branch of the CPUSA was answerable only to the Party leaders in New York, giving the Hollywood Communists an unusual degree of autonomy. From an initial membership of four screenwriters, the section grew to over one hundred members within a year and nearly three hundred within three years.[7]

Beginning in 1938, Martin Dies, Jr., the Democratic representative from Texas, had been holding federal hearings about his suspicion that communists had infiltrated Hollywood and other cultural institutions. Some of those hearings took place in Los Angeles in 1946. This federal probe, the House Committee on Un-American Activities, is commonly called HUAC (rather than HCUA), and it continued in different forms until the 1970s. It resulted in the "blacklisting" or banning from work about three hundred people named as communists, sympathetic to liberal ideas, or simply named by someone who wanted to label them as problematic. Walt testified in Washington at a HUAC hearing as a "friendly witness" at the instigation of another organization he belonged to, the Motion Picture Alliance for the Preservation of American Ideals.

Walt joined this organization in February 1944. The Motion Picture Alliance for the Preservation of American Ideals (called MPA, M.P.A., or Motion Picture Alliance) was a decidedly conservative political group with the purpose of defending America. In their statement of principles, the group starts out by saying, "We believe in, and like, the American way of life." Their goal is to show that the motion picture industry is not under the control of radicals: "In our special field of motion pictures, we resent the growing impression that this industry is made of, and dominated by, Communists, radicals, and crackpots," they stated. Their statement of purpose continued, "We refuse to permit the effort of Communist, Fascist, and other totalitarian-minded groups to pervert this powerful medium into an instrument for the dissemination of un-American ideas and beliefs."[8] Walt Disney was elected its first vice president.

In March 1944, the group sent a letter to North Carolina senator Robert R. Reynolds, thanking him for his support of pro-American ideas. This letter has been blamed for or credited with (depending on which side you were on) guiding Washington politicians to look at Hollywood in their search for communists. But it is clear from the earlier Tenney hearings and the Dies hearings that this was already happening. Nevertheless, the letter was a surprisingly frank appraisal of what the MPA considered an America under attack by aliens, alien ideologists, and their paid mercenaries. Citing Walt Disney as a member of the letter-writing group several times, the group complained about the "flagrant manner in which the motion-picture industrialists of Hollywood have been coddling Communists and cooperating with so-called intellectual superiors." They were tired of the people who were "smearing our leading patriots, and attempting to force us to surrender our birthright of individual as well as mass freedom to crackpot internationalists' schemes of a 'superduper' world government."[9] They signed the letter A GROUP OF YOUR FRIENDS IN HOLLYWOOD.

In October 1947, HUAC was looking at whether communists in Hollywood were planting propaganda in Hollywood movies and called 43 people to testify, 24 as "friendly" witness who could name others as communists, and 19 as "unfriendly" witnesses who were themselves under suspicion. The 19 unfriendly became 10 when some didn't appear or had some other reason for not testifying. After their testimony they became known as the Hollywood Ten, the ones who refused to answer the question of whether they were or had been members of the Communist Party.

This session of the hearings, which lasted nine days, was a follow-up to the earlier hearings both in Washington and Los Angeles; Walt did not testify at either of those. The committee noted that 85 million people attended the movies each year and that "it is the very magnitude of the scope of the motion-picture industry which makes this investigation so necessary."[10]

Other witnesses in October 1947 included some famous Hollywood personalities: actors George Murphy, Gary Cooper, and Robert Montgomery; author Ayn Rand; Ronald Reagan as head of the Screen Actors Guild; producers Louis B. Mayer and Jack Warner; and screenwriter Dalton Trumbo, who became one of the Hollywood Ten accused of being a communist. Warner, the head of production at Warner Bros., read a statement before his testimony (only friendly witnesses were allowed to read statements) which in part said:

> Our American way of life is under attack from without and from within our national borders. I believe it is the duty of each loyal American to resist those attacks and defeat them ...[11]

He called communists "ideological termites" and said he and his brothers would be willing to pay for "pest removal."[12] Other witnesses were just as colorful. Actor Adolphe Menjou, when asked if he thought members of the Screen Actors Guild were communists, said, "I know a great many people who act an awful lot like Communists."[13] He later continued, "I would move to the State of Texas, if it [communism] ever came here because I think Texans would kill them on sight."[14]

The Motion Picture Alliance was responsible for bringing to the witness stand many of the friendly witnesses including Walt Disney. Everyone was eventually asked to provide the names of known communists they worked with. The process became known as "naming names," identifying individuals whom the witness suspected of being a member of the Communist Party, having leftist leanings, or just being suspect because of something they said or did. The testimonies before Congress about the supposed communist infiltration of Hollywood was not about actually identifying the desired culprits. As Victor Navasky points out in his history of the HUAC and other hearings, "The HUAC hearings were degradation ceremonies. Their job was not to legislate or even to discover subversives (that had already been done by the intelligence agencies and their informants) so much as it was to stigmatize."[15] The hearings were more ceremonial than practical, a "surrealistic morality play" designed to prove that Congress was doing something about the perceived threat and that they could measure a person's character by whether they assisted the committee in its quest for cleaning up America.[16]

Walt testified before HUAC in October 1947 as a friendly witness, the same time as the Hollywood Ten. First he was asked if he thought movies could be used for propaganda purposes, and he admitted they could because he had successfully done that with his movie for the Treasury (*The New Spirit* in 1942 and the *Spirit of 43* in 1943), which got people to pay their taxes. He also cited his four anti-Hitler films as forms of propaganda.

Later in his testimony, he reiterated his claim that communists had instigated the strike at his studio and that Herbert Sorrell was to blame. Walt explained:

I believed at that time that Mr. Sorrell was a Communist because of all the things that I had heard and having seen his name

At microphone, movie cartoonist Walt Disney replies to questions of the House Un-American Activities Committee during a hearing of the communist probe in Washington, D.C., October 24, 1947. Disney told the group that a Hollywood union leader once said he could use the National Labor Relations Board "as it suited his purpose." (AP Photo)

appearing on a number of Commie front things. When he pulled the strike the first people to smear me and put me on the unfair list were all of the Commie front organizations. I can't remember them all, they change so often, but one that is clear in my mind is the League of Women Shoppers, The People's World, The Daily Worker, and the PM magazine in New York. They smeared me. Nobody came near to find out what the true facts of the thing were. And I even went through the same smear in South America, through some Commie periodicals in South America, and generally throughout the world all of the Commie groups began smear campaigns against me and my pictures.[17]

Walt was asked to name names by a member of the committee and he did:

Mr. SMITH: Can you name any other individuals that were active at the time of the strike that you believe in your opinion are Communists?

Mr. DISNEY: Well, I feel that there is one artist in my plant, that came in there, he came in about 1938, and he sort of stayed in the background, he wasn't too active, but he was the real brains of this, and I believe he is a Communist. His name is David Hilberman.

Mr. SMITH: How is it spelled?

Mr. DISNEY: H-i-l-b-e-r-m-a-n, I believe. I looked into his record and I found that, No. 1, that he had no religion and, No. 2, that he had considerable time at the Moscow Art Theater studying art direction, or something.

Mr. SMITH: Any others, Mr. Disney?

Mr. DISNEY: Well, I think Sorrell is sure tied up with them. If he isn't a Communist, he sure should be one.

Mr. SMITH: Do you remember the name of William Pomerance, did he have anything to do with it?

Mr. DISNEY: Yes, sir. He came in later. Sorrell put him in charge as business manager of cartoonists and later he went to the Screen Actors as their business agent and in turn he put in another man by the name of

Maurice Howard, the present business agent. And
they are all tied up with the same outfit.

Mr. SMITH: What is your opinion of Mr. Pomerance and Mr.
Howard as to whether or not they are or are not
Communists?

Mr. DISNEY: In my opinion they are Communists. No one has
any way of proving those things.[18]

Walt's testimony was described in the next day's *New York Times*
with the headline "Disney Denounces 'Communists'"[19] and was briefly
reported. Walt's move into anticommunism is usually explained by his
lingering bitterness about the 1941 strike. As one of his animators,
Ward Kimball, explained, "It hurt him because guys he trusted were
letting him down."[20] Walt considered himself the father of this happy
family, or the guy who created a productive and exciting community of
artists, and thought the strikers were "ingrates for calling a strike." It
didn't make sense to Walt that the problems that led to the strike were
internal rather than external.[21]

In some ways, this turn to anticommunism should seem odd. Walt
Disney was not a great capitalist. Walt was a man who said at various times that money was not important to him. What was important
was taking his ideas and making them real, using whatever money he
earned to jump-start the next quest. But to highlight just how murky
the consideration of this topic is, Walt was alternately praised by
the FBI for his anticommunist work and his positive portrayal of the
FBI in his media, and suspect as a communist sympathizer because of
some events he had attended (in his role as studio head) and some
people he associated with. Walt was designated a contact person
for FBI agents in his region, and he in turn had offered Disneyland
as a place for recreational events for the FBI and maybe even as a place
for its official operations. Yet nothing specific can be traced back to this
FBI connection other than some shows that highlighted the FBI.

Eric Johnston, head of the MPAA, testified that it was unfair to label
all Hollywood as influenced by communism and pointed out that the
committee never produced the list of communist-inspired films that
they always talked about (witnesses, however, named *Mission to Moscow* and *North Star* as examples, both from 1943). Johnston's advice to

the committee sounded surprisingly liberal in seeking a cause for the appeal of communism:

> The real breeding ground of communism is in the slums. It is everywhere where people haven't enough to eat or enough to wear through no fault of their own. Communism hunts misery, feeds on misery, and profits by it. Freedoms walk hand-in-hand with abundance. That has been the history of America. It has been the American story. It turned the eyes of the world to America, because America gave reality to freedom, plus abundance when it was still an idle daydream in the rest of the world.[22]

In November 1947, HUAC members voted to hold the Hollywood Ten in contempt because they would not recant or would not name names. They were all later sentenced to one year in jail after appeals were denied. Their names became the first on the blacklist when a group of studio executives met and drafted a statement that said that the Hollywood Ten would be banned from working in the industry and that the guilds needed to check the loyalty of their members. The opening of the statement, which was approved by all the producers present, not just those from the trade group mentioned (the Association of Motion Picture Producers) read:

> Members of the Association of Motion Picture Producers deplore the action of the 10 Hollywood men who have been cited for contempt by the House of Representatives. We do not desire to prejudge their legal rights, but their actions have been a disservice to their employers and have impaired their usefulness to the industry.
>
> We will forthwith discharge or suspend without compensation those in our employ, and we will not re-employ any of the 10 until such time as he is acquitted or has purged himself of contempt and declares under oath that he is not a Communist.
>
> On the broader issue of alleged subversive and disloyal elements in Hollywood, our members are likewise prepared to take positive action. We will not knowingly employ a Communist or a member of any party or group which advocates the overthrow of

the government of the United States by force or by any illegal or unconstitutional methods.[23]

The 10 blacklisted artists, who also appeared on lists published by the American Legion (a war veteran's group) and in a magazine called *Red Channels*,[24] as well as in the records of Congress and national magazines were joined in unemployment over the years by many more who were either named in other hearings or simply denied work by individual studios or guilds.[25] The HUAC hearings and the resulting blacklists affected Hollywood for years. Walt moved on to other things.

NOTES

1. Watts, Steven. *The Magic Kingdom: Walt Disney and the American Way of Life*. Boston: Houghton Mifflin, 1997, p. 273.

2. Ibid., pp. 274–80.

3. Gabler, Neal. *Walt Disney: The Triumph of the American Imagination*. New York: Knopf, 2006, p. 423.

4. Ibid., p. 425.

5. Thomas, Bob. *Walt Disney: An American Original*. New York: Hyperion, 1994, p. 204.

6. Gabler, p. 366.

7. Langdon, Jennifer E. *Caught in the Crossfire: Adrian Scott and the Politics of Americanism in 1940s Hollywood*. Columbia University Press, pp. 32–33. Available at http://www.gutenberg-e.org/langdon/chapter1.html. Accessed April 11, 2010.

8. *Hollywood Renegades Archives*. "The Motion Picture Alliance for the Preservation of American Ideals." Available at http://www.cobbles.com/simpp_archive/huac_alliance.htm. Accessed April 11, 2010.

9. Reynolds, Hon. Robert R. "Our Own First." 90 Cong. Rec. A1144 (1944) and Appendix—Extension of Remarks, 1944, p. A1143.

10. Committee on Un-American Activities. "Hearings Regarding the Communist Infiltration of the Motion-Picture Industry Activities in the United States." Hearing ID: Hrg-1947-Uah-0014. Document # Y4.Un1/2:C73/3. U.S. House of Representatives. Washington, D.C., October 20, 1947, p. 1.

11. Ibid., p. 9.

12. Ibid., p. 10.

13. Ibid., p. 94.

14. Ibid., p. 107.

15. Navasky, Victor S. *Naming Names*. New York: Penguin Books, 1980, p. 319.

16. Ibid., pp. vii–ix.

17. Committee on Un-American Activities. "Hearings Regarding the Communist Infiltration of the Motion-Picture Industry Activities in the United States." Hearing Id: Hrg-1947-Uah-0014. Document # Y4.Un1/2:C73/3. U.S. House of Representatives. Washington, D.C., October 20, 1947, p. 283. Most of the testimony is also available at http://historymatters.gmu.edu/d/6458. Accessed April 11, 2010.

18. Ibid., pp. 284–85.

19. Tower, Samuel. "Critics of Film Inquiry Assailed; Disney Denounces 'Communists'." *New York Times*, October 25, 1947, p.1.

20. Gabler, p. 366.

21. Ibid.

22. Committee on Un-American Activities, p. 308. The testimony is also available at http://www.terramedia.co.uk/reference/documents/johnston_evidence_to_huac.htm. Accessed April 11, 2010.

23. See the entire statement at http://www.answers.com/topic/waldorf-statement. Accessed April 11, 2010.

24. An issue of *Red Channels* can be seen at http://www.authentichistory.com/1946-1960/redchannels/redchannels.html. Accessed April 11, 2010.

25. See "Radio: Who's Blacklisted?" *Time*, August 22, 1949. Available at http://www.time.com/time/magazine/article/0,9171,800646,00.html. Accessed April 11, 2010.

Chapter 10

TRAINS

Whatever people thought about Walt Disney's adventure in pursuing communists after the war, they were still being presented with Disney productions that continued to provide entertainment and education through visual innovations and storytelling. The years after the war saw the beginning of Disney live-action films, the introduction of the *True-Life Adventure* nature documentaries, several animated features including a newly dubbed "classic," *Cinderella* (1950), a regular parade of cartoon shorts, and the first steps into television. The package features (combinations of short films and cartoons) the studio was putting together were somewhat successful, and merchandise licensing was expanding so the studio's books didn't look too bad after a while. Walt also began thinking about a new kind of amusement park for families to enjoy themselves.

In August of 1947 (before his HUAC testimony), Walt and his daughter Sharon took a trip to Alaska, which he considered one of the final frontiers. After he came back, he saw a wildlife movie by the husband-and-wife team, Alfred and Elma Milotte. Walt liked what he saw and hired them to shoot more footage in Alaska, where they lived. When he saw scenes from the Pribilof Islands in the Bering Sea containing seal life, he asked them to focus on that. Out of their work came the first *True-Life Adventure*, a series of nature films that developed into a profitable and popular award-winning series for the studio. The Milottes spent another decade shooting films all over the world. The first film in the series, *Seal Island*, was completed in 1948, and Walt wanted RKO to distribute it. When they weren't interested, he created a one-week showing at a friend's theatre so it could qualify for an Academy Award. The film won an Oscar for best short subject and also garnered other important awards. It was released to the public in the spring of 1949.

Contrary to common descriptions of the *True-Life Adventures*, they were not the first ever nature documentaries. The natural world had been a common subject in early cinema, including Edweard Muybridge's work with animal locomotion, and time-lapse images of flowers and butterfly metamorphosis by other artists.[1] Nature films showing animal life, landscapes, and natural events were captured on film by other early filmmakers. But what Walt did was "unite the disparate elements of wildlife filmmaking up to that time, consolidated them in a unified but still flexible form, and above all popularized them as never before."[2] He did this by giving the hours of raw footage he was presented with a narrative form, a story that was as recognizable as the ones from his cartoons. He also made these stories familiar ones of loving family life, persevering in the face of hardships, or basic good versus evil.

The *True-Life Adventures* used music and humorous scenes to give the animals personalities and for this it was both criticized and praised. Seven short and six full-length features were created between 1948 and 1960, and together they earned eight Academy Awards. While Walt claimed the films were representations of the natural world, they were like many later nature films, taking selective scenes and emphasizing the interesting or anthropomorphic action where the animals seemed most human. Walt seemed to favor the natural over the human worlds when he said, "In one way, you know, animals are superior to human beings. People try to change nature to conform to their own queer notions. Animals don't—they adapt themselves to nature. You never saw a wilderness wrecked by animals."[3]

Walt got interested in nature films and the realistic world of animal life when the studio was working with live animals as models when animating *Bambi,* but he didn't follow up on the ideas for live-action nature films until after the war. For Walt, the stories constructed in the nature films naturally built on the animations he had been doing for 30 years. He explained in an interview, "You know why the animals dominate animated cartoons? It's because their reaction to any kind of stimulus is expressed physically. Often the entire body comes into play ... But how does a human being react to a stimulus? He's lost the sense of play he once had, and he inhibits physical expression."[4] In the early *True-Life Adventures,* all human presence was hidden, but later on they became the subject of the films in a series called *People and Places.*

One *True-Life Adventure* film, *White Wilderness* (1958), may have been less true-to-life than the others. In that film, winner of an Academy Award and shot in the coldest of Arctic habitats by nine photographers for three years, animals are shown migrating and battling for dominance. One scene that became controversial and also the basis of an urban legend was one in which lemmings flung themselves off a cliff in a suicidal drive, providing "an unwitting sacrifice for the few left behind."[5] The scene was famous and references to lemmings as an example of blindly following the crowd are still common today. But lemmings don't normally exhibit this type of behavior, wildlife experts explained years later, and they did not doubt that the scene was set up by the filmmakers themselves.[6]

The *True-Life Adventure* films resulted in a series of books and comic books, television segments, and a lasting influence on nature documentaries. At its height, the series had 30–40 film crews going at once around the world. The films were shown on television and in schools across the country. Although Walt had decided after the war not to focus on educational or instructional films as he had done during the war, the *True-Life Adventures* certainly ended up being a widespread educational tool. They also were very popular in both their short and long versions. When Disney's distributor, RKO, hesitated to show the first long nature feature, *The Living Desert* in 1953, Roy and Walt developed their own distribution company, Buena Vista, which became known for its family fare and continues to this day as a Disney distributor.

The Living Desert, which is about the harsh but abundant life in desert environments, went on to win the Academy Award for best documentary (feature) in the 1954 award ceremony for films of 1953. Walt also won an unprecedented three additional awards the same year: for the best documentary (short subject) for *The Alaskan Eskimo* (a *People and Places* featurette); the best short subject (cartoon) for *Toot, Whistle, Plunk and Boom*, which was about music and was developed by Ward Kimball with an innovative animation style; and the best short subject (two-reel) for *Bear Country*, a *True-Life Adventure* featurette. In addition, two of his other films received nominations. In fact, he received nominations for something that came out of his studio every year except one between 1932 and his death in 1966. Walt is quoted as saying about the *True-Life Adventures*, "Nothing in a lifetime of picture making has been more exciting and personally satisfactory than these delvings in to the wonders, the mysteries, the magnificent common-places of life around us and passing them on via the screen."[7] Not only had Walt proven that he had not lost his imagination or his drive, but he was not yet finished with on-screen innovation.

Part of the difficulty in getting the Disney studio back up and running was the fact that some of its much-needed money was tied up in Europe. European banks blocked the funds that Disney movies had earned. This means that the money, because of regulations put in place to control how money leaves the host country during and after the war, could not be used in the United States. Money that was earned in Great Britain, for example, had to be used there or forfeited or converted at great loss. Walt had thought about opening an animation studio in England as a way to use the funds but opted instead to try his hand at producing live-action films.

The live-action films, along with the *True-Life Adventures*, may have created the impression that the studio was moving away from anima-tions. But instead it could be seen as adding to the repertoire of sto-rytelling techniques and media that was fast becoming the hallmark of the postwar Disney studio. The first story Walt chose for his live-action debut was *Treasure Island* (1950), a classic tale of pirates and treasure based on the book by Robert Louis Stevenson. It was the first of four live-action films made overseas. Walt supervised the postpro-duction work on the movie, and it was both popular and successful, generating funds for the studio and opening up new creative possibili-ties. *Treasure Island* was followed by *The Story of Robin Hood and His*

Merrie Men (1952), *The Sword and the Rose* (1953), and *Rob Roy, the Highland Rogue* (1954). After the four blocked-fund pictures, production returned to the United States, and some Disney features drew on *True-Life Adventures* for inspiration (*Old Yeller* in 1957, for example) as well as animations, with some becoming combined animations and live action (most notably *Mary Poppins* in 1964) and others using innovative special effects (*The Absent-Minded Professor* in 1961).

The next film in the new enterprise for the Disney studio was a Jules Verne tale called *20,000 Leagues under the Sea*. Released in 1954 after live production returned to the United States, it featured some of the most famous stars of the day including Kirk Douglas, James Mason, and Peter Lorre. It became the most expensive film the studio had invested in up to that time, and it paid back handsomely. It also used a

Walt Disney and his family arrive from a three-month trip abroad via TWA Constellation at Los Angeles, California, on August 1949. He is posing with his wife, Lillian, left, and their daughters Diane, 16, and Sharon, 13, right. Disney was supervising filming of the movie Treasure Island *in London. (AP Photo)*

production tool of the animations that the studio had been producing for years: the storyboard, which was detailed and novel at the time for live-action films. The studio had its own sound stages for production but also built new ones to accommodate the project.

In a lovely irony, Walt hired as his director Richard Fleischer, the son of his long-ago animation rival Max Fleischer whose studio made the *Out of the Inkwell* cartoons. Fleischer checked with his father to make sure it was okay. The film won Academy Awards both for its special effects and its sets and art direction. The film features an exotic Nautilus, Captain Nemo's submarine, as well as a fabulous squid that attacked the ship and real underwater sequences. Other live-action films also used advanced special effects over the years, some of them developed by Ub Iwerks.

The Disney studio and its subsidiaries became known through the subsequent years for live-action films that presented family-appropriate comedies, dramas, and adventure films frequently set in past ages.

Walt Disney, who had won 22 Oscars previously, holds the two he accepted March 30, 1955, at the Annual Academy Awards presentations in Hollywood, California. Disney won for the best special effects and best art direction in 20,000 Leagues under the Sea. (AP Photo)

These were often considered silly and sentimental by many critics, but they have gained many new fans through the years. Among the most notable that were created before Walt's death were *The Shaggy Dog* (1959), *Kidnapped* (1960), *Pollyanna* (1960), *The Parent Trap* (1961), *In Search of the Castaways* (1962), and *The Moon Spinners* (1964). The last four films starred a young actress, Hayley Mills, who became one of the biggest child stars of the time. Mills remembers Walt as a gentle and shy man who had a goal for all his films: "He always said his films were to remind people of the goodness in human beings," she said.[8]

If Walt really came from frontier stock, then his next steps into uncharted territory would be the test of his resolve. Television was developed in the early part of the 20th century. A television concept was proposed at the World's Fair in Paris in 1900, and by 1939 television sets were being displayed at the New York World's Fair (along with Mickey Mouse watches). After the war, millions of homes acquired televisions, and within a few years there were numerous stations and half the nation was watching TV. Walt had been watching the developments in television and saw an opportunity. In 1950, he created a Christmas special called *One Hour in Wonderland*. The show was basically an advertisement for the upcoming feature animation, *Alice in Wonderland*, which was released the next summer. In 1951, he developed another Christmas special, *Walt Disney Christmas Show*, which was essentially a promotional piece for the next animation, *Peter Pan*, which opened in 1953 but had been in production for several years already.

Walt had hit upon a formula that would develop into one of the longest running shows on television beginning in 1954. He used a combination of sneak previews for his upcoming films and other ventures combined with nature films, travelogues, science segments, cartoons, original programming (like the *Davy Crockett* shows), and movies. The production of *20,000 Leagues under the Sea* was featured on one show. Walt was the host, and he was welcomed into millions of homes Sunday nights, first with a show titled *Disneyland*, then *Walt Disney Presents*, then a show titled *Walt Disney's Wonderful World of Color* to take advantage of color broadcasting in 1961, and finally *The Wonderful World of Disney*. Watching Walt Disney with his gentle demeanor and plain talking was a weekly ritual across the country.

With all these new ventures underway in the late 1940s and early 1950s, it seems hard to insist that Walt wasn't committed to his work. But if anyone was still thinking that Walt had lost his way, they could find evidence in two of his newly evident hobbies: miniatures and trains. Walt, like thousands of hobbyists in the postwar period, became fascinated with the creation, collection, and display of miniature scenes, furniture, and rooms as well as model train sets. Walt's interest in trains went way back but found new expression in the development of actual train models of different scales.

Critics think this was Walt's attempt to get control of his life. Tracing this to his deepest personality traits, biographer Neal Gabler claimed that Walt was trying to "create an even better fortress for himself," and proving that he had the ability to craft "a better reality," one that would be in his control.[9] To Gabler, control was the key term to explain Walt during this period. He explained that the miniatures were another way "for Walt to assert his control at the very time he seemed to be losing it."[10] But attempts to control or organize the world in our own image are not a psychological flaw as Gabler seems to suggest. It is instead what all humans do, all the time. Walt, in this sense, is doing the most human of activities: creating a miniature world, only this time not just in his head or on the screen, but right there in front of him. It was, perhaps, a necessary step toward visualizing the new amusement park he had started thinking about.

What is the appeal of "life in a nutshell" or "in the palm of your hands" as many miniature enthusiasts describe their mini-worlds? Miniature enthusiasts display scenes using houses or events that are captured in time and space, but there is more than nostalgia and control going on here. These worlds are not fixed and can be considered a starting point for fantasy, for imagining all sorts of possibilities. As a form of play, which adults as well as children engage in, miniatures are a way of trying out the world, seeing how it can be put together, what aspects of it fit, and what needs to be reworked. This is not therapy, but an everyday process we all engage in by different means, whether it is miniatures or movies, board games or vacations. It is a direct route to a sense of wonder, to the domain of magic where anything is possible, or where we can imagine things we haven't yet seen. Miniature worlds are fantasy made concrete. Walt was not trying to regain the control he lost but was finding ways of sharing his sense of wonder with the rest of us.

Walt started collecting and creating miniatures; furniture, musical instruments, table settings, tea sets, accessories, and entire scenes.
Miniatures were popular displays at that time. He could have seen the
famous Thorne collection of miniature rooms (now residing at The Art
Institute of Chicago) at the 1939–40 World's Fair in New York or at the
1939 expo in San Francisco, but they were also displayed at museums
throughout the West Coast in the same period. Walt collected and created miniatures for several years and during his travels sought out miniature shows and shops and purchased things through advertisements.
One scene he created was called "Granny's Cabin" and it consisted of
a miniature set from the combined live-action/animation film *So Dear
to My Heart,* which was released in 1949. Walt displayed the scene at
Festival of California Living in Los Angeles, which was held at the
Pan-Pacific Auditorium, a huge indoor exhibition space (the famous
façade of that now burned-down building provided inspiration for the
façade designs at later Disney theme parks). The model recently went
on display at Disney World and the tag describing the object states,
"Hand-built by Walt Disney himself, this animated diorama was an
early attempt at dimensional storytelling, and helped inspire the concept for Disneyland Park four years later."

Miniatures, in classic Disney style, weren't just a personal indul-
gence. Walt had a plan as his collection expanded and "dimensional
storytelling" was a good way to describe it. He was going to display the
scenes, which depicted moments in the life of America, in an innovative exhibit called "Disneylandia." Disneylandia was first conceived as
taking place in a traveling train. The train would come into a town
and the visitors would enter to view the miniature dioramas. Walt put
some of his artists to work on the displays, but the logistics of moving the train around the country and getting an audience proved hard
to overcome. The ideas behind the displays, however, eventually got
translated into bigger things, and the train went with it.

Trains were a long-time interest of Walt's. From his early days in
Marceline when his Uncle Mike engineered on the local rails to his
summer work selling refreshments on a train, to the one-way trip to
California, and all the trips between the East and West Coasts as he
sold his ideas and eventually created Mickey Mouse, trains have always
been a favored form of transport for Walt. But trains also held the same
fascination that miniatures did, and Walt's commitment to them was

even more passionate. Before Christmas in 1947, Walt wrote to his sister Ruth that he had bought himself an electric train, which he set up in a room outside his office. He told Ruth it was something he wanted all his life and added, "It's just wonderful."[11]

Two of Walt's loyal animators from the Nine Old Men group, Ollie Johnston and Ward Kimball, came over to look at the set, and Walt found in them two men who shared the same passion for trains. Johnston explained, "Out of that we had quite a close relationship."[12] Johnston had built miniature trains and started running them in his yard around 1946. Kimball created and collected scale trains too, and both Johnston and Kimball eventually had life-size trains on their home properties that Walt came over to visit. Kimball also developed one of the best and largest private collections of miniature trains.

Walt invited Ward Kimball to accompany him to visit the Chicago Railroad Fair in the summer of 1948. They took a train from California, and once there they got a chance to ride on vintage trains and view the historic exhibits. Kimball reported that Walt was thrilled by the entire experience, including showing his employee how he used to ride the Chicago elevated trains.[13] The 50 acres of the fair, which was celebrating 100 years of western railroad history, were like a railroad world's fair with parades, technology displays, and themed activity areas including an Indian village, a frontier mining town, and New Orleans's French Quarter.[14] Walt apparently got talked into appearing in one of the historic reenactments. Walt and Ward also visited Greenfield Village, one of the largest outdoor museums. Located in Dearborn, Michigan, Greenfield Village focused on Americana and contained actual and reproduction historical buildings including Thomas Edison's lab.

When Walt got back, he worked on scale model trains, which he learned how to make himself. He also had plans for a scaled yard train like Johnston's and Kimball's and he hired several skilled workers to help him on that. Walt and Lilly were looking for property to build a new home around this time, and Walt made sure it had enough room for his model train, which circled the property on a half-mile track. Walt called the train Lilly Belle after Lilly who was not entirely enthusiastic about the project. He called his backyard one-eighth scale rail line the Carolwood Pacific after the street he lived on. He erected a barn, said to be modeled after the one on his family farm in Marceline, to house his equipment; the barn was eventually moved to Griffith Park in Los Angeles where it can still be seen.

On the train back from Chicago and Dearborn, Walt did some writing. It seems that Walt was not only enjoying the railroad fair, he was getting ideas from it, ideas on how to put together his next great adventure. Not only was Walt interested in the trains, he also "scanned the flow of people from one exhibit to another," watched how the food was prepared, and generally surveyed the way to entertain and organize large numbers of people.[15] He sketched out the plans for a fun, clean, and interesting place and he sent these in an internal memo to one of his designers at the end of August 1948. It was the plan for Mickey Mouse Park, which would be located across the street from the studio and would give visitors something to do besides watch the animators.

The memo, however, was describing more than just an extension of a studio tour. It revealed a plan for an entire world devoted to a new form of amusement park. The park would have a village center with a train station and town hall, places to sit and watch the children: "I want it to be very relaxing, cool and inviting" the memo said. The village would have a police and fire station; a candy store, Disney merchandise store, and dollhouse shop; a soda fountain; and places for food. It would feature a wild west and Indian village area, a farm, and a carnival.

So now the trains, and the miniatures, television programs, the family-oriented live-action films, the latest animated myths, all these illusions of, and allusions to, life were all headed for the same place. The fun rides around the backyard on mini-sized trains, the nature films, the return of Ub Iwerks, the Railroad Fair, the visits to World's Fairs and amusement parks, and the new special effects technologies all seemed to be fulfilling one goal. All tracks, all thoughts, all roads were leading one place: they were going, finally, to Mickey Mouse Park.

NOTES

1. Bouse, Derek. *Wildlife Films*. Philadelphia: University of Pennsylvania Press, 2000, p. 57.

2. Ibid., p. 62.

3. Sampson, Wade. "In Walt's Worlds: Natural Walt." January 30, 2008. Available at http://www.mouseplanet.com/8233/In_Walts_Worlds_Natural_Walt. Accessed April 11, 2010.

4. Alexander, Jack. "The Amazing Story of Walt Disney, Conclusion." *Saturday Evening Post*, November 7, 1953, p. 27.

5. Jungmeyer, Jack. "Filming a 'Wilderness.'" *New York Times*, August 3, 1958.

6. Yoon, Carol Kaesuk. "Scientists Find Lemmings Die as Dinner, Not Suicides." *New York Times*, October 31, 2003, p. A10.

7. "True to Life." *Walt Disney Archives*. Available at http://d23.disney.go.com/articles/042209_NF_FS_TrueLife.html. Accessed April 11, 2010.

8. "Interview with Hayley Mills." *The Walt Disney Family Museum*. Available at http://disney.go.com/disneyatoz/familymuseum/exhibits/familyfriends/hayleymills/index.html. Accessed April 11, 2010.

9. Gabler, Neal. *Walt Disney: The Triumph of the American Imagination*. New York: Knopf, 2006, pp. 479–81.

10. Ibid., p. 481.

11. Barrier, Michael. *The Animated Man: A Life of Walt Disney*. Berkeley: University of California Press, 2007, p. 209.

12. Canemaker, John. *Walt Disney's Nine Old Men & the Art of Animation*. New York: Disney Editions, 2001, p. 224.

13. Ibid., p. 112.

14. See a program for the second year of the fair, "Chicago Railroad Fair 1949." Available at http://www.railarchive.net/rrfair/index.html. Accessed April 11, 2010.

15. Greene, Katherine and Richard Greene. *The Man Behind the Magic: The Story of Walt Disney*. New York: Viking Penguin, 1991, p. 110.

Chapter 11

THE MAGIC KINGDOM

In July 1956, the Barstow family gathered in front of their Wethersfield, Connecticut, home for some news, and a home-movie camera captured a remarkable scene. A telegram had arrived, and the news in it made first Robbins Barstow dramatically faint and then his wife Meg, and then each of their kids: Mary, David, and Daniel. They had won a contest, and the prize was a free family trip to Disneyland. The home movie that showed their preparations for the contest, their exaggerated surprise at winning, and their subsequent trip to the Magic Kingdom is the delightful production of amateur filmmaker Robbins Barstow. The wonderful editing and storytelling won the film a place in the National Film Registry in 2008, a Library of Congress designation that preserves culturally, historically, or aesthetically significant films (*Steamboat Willie* from 1928 and *Snow White and the Seven Dwarfs* from 1937 are also on the list).[1]

The Barstow family had achieved a dream that was shared by more than one million other people who entered the contest, which was sponsored by the 3M company (they made Scotch Brand cellophane tape). The contest was one of many promotional activities tied to the rerelease of the combined live-action/animation film *Song of the South*, which was first released in 1946 and received negative reviews then. The contest was called the "Brer Rabbit's Zip-A-Dee-Doo-Dah Contest," and it required completing the following sentence in 25 words or less: "I like 'SCOTCH' Brand Cellophane Tape because ..." The winning Barstow family entry was by young Danny, age four, who wrote, "I like "SCOTCH" Brand Tape because when some things tear then I can just use it. Danny." Twenty-four other families won as well.

The Barstows dressed in their homemade Davy Crockett jackets, and when they made it to Disneyland, they had completed their "family dream journey." By 1956, the Disneyland park was now filled with many more completed rides than when the park first opened, and the Barstows received four days worth of tickets for the attractions. Their film documents the early days of Disneyland from the viewpoint of visitors and shows the early connections between the rides at Disneyland and the Disney movies, cartoons, and characters that were presented in them, including a ride with *Snow White and the Seven Dwarfs*, a *Dumbo* ride, the tea cups from *Alice in Wonderland*, and the whale from *Pinocchio*. It also shows that Walt translated his love of miniatures into a display of tiny settings from fairy tales and his love of trains into several attractions including the "Casey, Jr., Circus Train."

Perhaps every story of Walt Disney's life should really begin at Disneyland. It is here at the theme park that we can see, in concrete form, the years and years of Walt's imaginative thinking and creative storytelling. The facility the Barstows visited in 1956 was far more advanced and exciting than the planned Mickey Mouse Park that Walt had outlined in 1948 and had been thinking about for years. But the translation of Mickey Mouse Park into Disneyland was complex and seemingly doomed to failure from the start. All sorts of stories exist about how Walt got the idea for Disneyland, and most of them mention that he would sit passively while watching his daughters enjoying rides at a local park during weekend outings. In the story, Walt is always thinking that the entire family should have a place where they can have fun together in an environment that was clean, safe, attracted normal people, and had a friendly staff.

Research on different kinds of attractions and parks had been part of Walt's activities for a long time, and he also sent some of his staff out to existing amusement parks to see how they functioned and what was good and bad about them. Walt's friend Art Linkletter remembered that when they visited Tivoli Gardens in Denmark in 1951, Walt took notes on everything: the lights, the seats, the food. When Linkletter asked what he was doing, Walt explained that he was making notes for a "great playground" for kids and their families.[2] But Disneyland can be traced to more than just a perceived need for clean and safe family amusement. Certainly the World's Fairs that had a role in so many aspects of Walt's life came into play, as did Greenfield Village and the Chicago Railroad Fair of 1948. They each provided a model of how to move people about, keep them busy and entertained, provide them with a quality experience, and get them to buy merchandise. But they also were showing an idealized world where advances in technology lived beside a respect for the past. They each provided an entire world, like the miniature dioramas, that encapsulated an entire imaginative universe, and Disneyland, as its name implies, was going to do the same thing for Walt's worldview.

Walt's interest in trains may have provided an early structure for the park because no matter what, a train track was going to circumnavigate the land. Walt's interest in miniature settings honed his skills in three-dimensional storytelling, and the movies, cartoons, comic books, storybooks, and merchandise integrated known characters and material culture into a fully realized alternative world, a Magic Kingdom, the land for everything Disney had come to represent. Disneyland, as many have noted over the decades, was Walt's dreams made real, the years of work on screen-based fantasies turned into tangible experience and a sense-oriented place beyond just sight and sound. Disneyland was not the first amusement park, but it became the prototype. The power of the prototype is that you set the model and the rules and everyone else has to respond in relation to what you have done.

Not everyone liked the world built by Walt and for some the rise of Disneyland sealed that opinion. A few years after the opening, an article in the Nation complained that "As in the Disney movies, the whole world, the universe, and all man's striving for dominion over self and nature, have been reduced to a sickening blend of cheap formulas packaged to sell. Romance, Adventure, Fantasy, Science are ballyhooed and marketed: life is bright colored, clean, cute, titivating, safe, mediocre, inoffensive to the lowest common denominator, and somehow poignantly inhuman. ... The invitation and challenge of real living is abandoned. ... The overwhelming feeling that one carries away is sadness for the empty lives which accept such tawdry substitutes."[3] Walt's friend Ray Bradbury was angry about this comment and wrote this response to the editor: "The world is full of people who, for intellectual reasons, steadfastly refuse to let go and enjoy themselves ... I found, in Disneyland, vast reserves of imagination before untapped in our country ... I feel sorry for him.[4]

It was always said about Walt that he didn't care about making money except as it was necessary for him to put into effect his next project, so it always fell to Roy to work out the finances. Roy did not like the idea of Mickey Mouse Park and neither did Lilly. It was going to be too expensive, hard to sell as an idea to backers, and why bother going in a new direction? But for Walt it was not just another business venture. It was a chance to build the "Happiest Place on Earth."

Walt put his own money together to start the project. He established a separate company that came to be known as WED (his initials) in 1952, and it was devoted to developing Disneyland. The people working at WED became "Imagineers," and they needed the combination of imagination and engineering to pull the project off. In 1953, Walt met with the artist Herb Ryman (a past but not current employee) and together they sketched a visual plan for Disneyland in one weekend (other preliminary sketches were done earlier). They needed to have plans ready for Roy to take to New York on Monday to show to the television networks that they hoped would fund the venture. The conceptual image created by Ryman as Walt talked about his dream park was a schematic aerial view that showed all the lands and details of specific attractions including Sleeping Beauty's castle, the Mark Twain boat, the train that ran around the park, and Tomorrowland architecture.

Both NBC and CBS, the two major networks of the day, passed on the proposal Roy took to them, which included funding of the park in exchange for a television show by Walt. ABC, however, made the deal. They invested half a million dollars and cosigned a loan for four and a half million more. In return they received 35 percent ownership of Disneyland and a weekly show from Walt. Disneyland took one year and 17 million dollars to build, with the rest of the money coming from loans and investors who got on board the Disneyland train after they saw Walt's presentation of it in the television series.

Walt Disney sits on a rock in front of the Sleeping Beauty Castle in the Fantasyland section of Disneyland on July 17, 1995, opening day of the amusement theme park in Anaheim, California. (AP Photo)

The first television show for ABC presented under the contract, called *Disneyland*, opened with "The Disneyland Story," which aired October 27, 1954. Walt begins the show with an acknowledgement of Mickey Mouse when he says, "Guess you all know this little fellow here (nodding in the direction of a Mickey Mouse picture). It's an old partnership. ... We've had a lot of our dreams come true." Walt described his vision, saying Disneyland would be "unlike anything else on this earth: a fair, an amusement park, an exhibition, a city from Arabian nights, a metropolis from the future. In fact, a place of hopes and dream, fact and fancy, all in one." He also reminded viewers of the importance of Mickey Mouse later in the show: "Our only hope is we never lose sight of one thing: that it was all started by a mouse. Now, that is why I want this part of the show to belong to Mickey, because the story of Mickey is truly the real beginning of Disneyland."[5]

The show described the hub design of the park with the four worlds—Adventureland, Tomorrowland, Frontierland, and Fantasyland—going off in four directions at the end of Main Street. Frontierland had burro and stagecoach rides and the "Mark Twain Riverboat," evoking the push west that was part of American lore; Tomorrowland had a rocket-ship to the moon and science displays; Adventureland played off of the *True-Life Adventures* series and offered a jungle boat ride with mechanical animals; Fantasyland featured Disney cartoons and characters as inspirations for attractions including Captain Hook's pirate ship and Snow White's adventure. "Main Street, USA" was a scaled-down version of Marceline, Missouri's main street.

The television series later that year introduced Davy Crockett, and the country was seized by a Davy Crockett craze that was reflected in the jackets and coonskin hats worn by the Barstow family. Fess Parker as Davy Crockett appeared at the dedication ceremonies for Disneyland with Buddy Ebsen as his sidekick. Several other episodes featured developments at the park and another show, the *Mickey Mouse Club*, started airing afternoons on October 3, 1955. It, too, was designed to promote Disneyland but it became a cultural phenomenon and like the original Mickey Mouse clubs in the early 1930s it provided a way to be part of the Disney world. The teen cast was known as Mouseketeers, and they became famous across the country. They performed at the Mickey Mouse Club Circus in Disneyland the first year the park was open.

Perhaps Walt's commitment to the place can be best understood by a story told about evangelist Billy Graham's first visit to Disneyland in the early 1960s. Getting off the Jungle Cruise ride, Graham is reported to have said to Walt, "What a marvelous fantasy world!" Walt is said to have replied, "Billy, look around you at all the people. All the nationalities. All the colors. All the languages. All of them smiling. All of them having fun together. Billy, *this* is the *real* world. The fantasy's outside."[6] The ability to make a new reality is a wonderful power and through all his other productions on the screen Walt succeeded in approaching this goal. That he was now able to do this in the world of reality, or to make his world more real, more important, more desired than reality itself, was an almost incomprehensible accomplishment.

It was the "eighth wonder of the world" reported Hedda Hopper, a Hollywood columnist who covered Walt and Lilly's 30th anniversary party, which was held at Disneyland a few days before the park opened. But to her it was also the "ninth, tenth, eleventh and twelfth" as well. Even though their stay in the park was short, she said of the experience "we all went home with the feeling of having been reborn."[7]

July 17, 1955, was hot. The opening ceremonies on this preview day for the new type of amusement park Walt Disney had created were presented to Americans through a live broadcast to 90 million people. The 29 live cameras were intercut with prerecorded segments that showed the guests, some celebrities (Ronnie Reagan, Frank Sinatra, Sammy Davis, Art Linkletter, Fess Parker, Buddy Ebsen, Danny Thomas) and the opening parade. Walt was featured reading a dedication for each section of the park. The crowd of about 15,000 invited guests and up to 20,000 unexpected extra ones saw a park that had about 20 attractions and many incomplete areas. Rides were crowded or broke down, lines were long, and trash ended up all over the park. By the end of the day,

Governor Goodwin J. Knight, of California, center; Walt Disney, left; and Fred G. Gurley, president of Santa Fe Railroad, right, board the cab of an old-time railroad engine to take a ride around Disneyland in Anaheim, California, July 17, 1955. Disneyland, 160 acres and 17 million dollars of fun, opened its doors that day. (AP Photo)

most of the "Autopia" cars were crashed or broken while the rest of Tomorrowland just wasn't even open.

The heat and lack of water fountains (due to a plumbers strike) and other opening day glitches seemed to overwhelm some impressions of that day. But visitors still encountered an unprecedented experience. The *Los Angeles Times* finished their coverage of the dedication ceremony with the statement "It was the end of the first day's chapter in the new magic world of Disneyland."[8] The *New York Times*, however, in a critical commentary a few weeks after the park opened, saw Disneyland as just another roadside attraction that detached visitors from their money. The only difference was that Walt created his amusement park by utilizing his "lifelong forte of peddling illusion."[9]

The simple goal of making people happy, whatever that meant, did seem to be the message Walt wanted to convey by Disneyland. On the plaque commemorating Walt's words on opening day is the following statement:

To all who come to this happy place:
WELCOME.
Disneyland is your land.
Here age relives fond memories of the past . . .
and here youth may savor the challenge and promise of the future.
Disneyland is dedicated to the ideals, the dreams, and the hard facts that have created America . . . with the hope that it will be a source of joy and inspiration to all the world.

The next day, when the park was opened to the public, thousands of people arrived. The *Los Angeles Times* reported the problems matter-of-factly, explaining that "the opening day crowds were tremendous and nearly everyone expressed awe, satisfaction and enjoyment in spite of the hot sun, the elbow-to-elbow throng and the breakdowns."[10] Disneyland was on its way to being one of the most popular family destinations in the country. Admission at this time was one dollar for adults (Roy Disney purchased the first ticket as a keepsake) and attractions were priced individually from 10 cents to 35 cents with ticket purchase at each ride. Ticket books were instituted in October of that first year and had designations of "A" to "C" depending on the price of the ride. "E" tickets were introduced in 1959 when the park added several spectacular rides including the "Matterhorn Bobsleds," a themed rollercoaster. The expression "'E' ticket ride" became a general way in the wider culture of explaining that something was of excellent quality.

Despite the early problems, the park expanded and improved and within a few months one million people had visited. Disneyland became world-famous and the park became a required destination for distinguished visitors to the United States, including many foreign heads of state as well as the country's own famous and powerful. By the time the Barstows arrived one year after the opening, more than three and a half million people had entered the Magic Kingdom. A press release on the first anniversary stated that "in keeping with Walt Disney's policy, the Park will continue to expand and refine its operation to offer unparalleled entertainment to its millions of visitors each year." Its attraction list now totaled 33 and Disney's (second) "folly" had proven itself. The favorite rides were listed as "the Peter Pan dark ride in Fantasyland, the Adventureland Jungle River Boat Ride, the Santa Fe and Disneyland trains, and the Autopia Freeway's miniature autos in Tomorrowland."[11] Other attractions that were open included the "Golden Horseshoe Revue," "Circarama, U.S.A." (a 360-degree movie playing A *Tour of the West*), "Dumbo Flying Elephants," and the "Aluminum Hall of Fame."

Through the years, new attractions were added to the park, each reflecting advances in technology, new concepts in storytelling, replacements for failed rides, or new Disney movies and animations. For example, "Swiss Family Treehouse" opened in 1962, based on the 1960 movie *Swiss Family Robinson*. The "Rainbow Cavern Mine Train" and the "Caverns of Rainbow Mountain" (developed in the first few years) were derived from the *True-Life Adventures*. Walt's daughter Diane explained in 1957 that "Dad is always taking Disneyland apart and putting it back together in a new way." Walt in the same interview said about Disneyland, "I've always wanted to work on something that keeps on growing, and I've got that in Disneyland."[12] To him it was a living, organic place that developed on its own and matured with his help. It would continue to grow, he said, "as long as there is imagination left in the world."[13] It was, he often said, a work of love.

Meanwhile, the Disney studio continued to produce live-action features, animations, television programs (including a new, popular series, *Zorro*), and *True-Life Adventures*. The feature animation *Sleeping Beauty* was released in 1959, and the first live-action comedy, *The Shaggy Dog* (about a boy who magically gets turned into a dog), was released in 1959 also with great success at the box office. The next year saw, besides *Swiss Family Robinson*, the release of several more films including the now classic *Pollyanna* with Hayley Mills. *Mary Poppins* was released in 1964, and it combined live-action and animation with great success. Walt was involved closely with the project and contributed ideas and comments on a regular basis. The film received 13 Academy Award nominations, including best picture, and Julie Andrews won for best actress.

Walt and Roy began looking into the feasibility of building a Disneyland on the East Coast. Even though Disneyland had already attracted visitors from all the states and dozens of foreign countries, it was mainly a regional attraction. Walt had also gotten involved with the February 1960 Winter Olympics which were held in California. He was Chairman of Pageantry and was in charge of both Opening and Closing Ceremonies, which featured 5,000 participants. The ceremonies were not as elaborate as they are today. The Opening Ceremony was outdoors and indoors, and included the release of birds and balloons as well as skiers and a skater bringing in the Olympic torch. Disney also provided 32 large snow sculptures to decorate the area, a design for the Olympic torch, and entertainment for the participants.

The opportunity to help Disneyland make a huge leap in its technological and storytelling achievements was advanced by Walt's work with the 1964–65 New York World's Fair. Like the other fairs in history, this one was designed to show the world that the host city was worthy of the honor of accommodating the technological and social advances displayed by the participants. New York was celebrating its 300th anniversary and while this was not an officially sanctioned World's Fair according to the international rules, it was a big, celebrated event that attracted major participants and 51 million visitors.

Walt saw an opportunity to do several things: try out Disney ideas on an East Coast audience; generate money by working for large corporations and designing their exhibits; focus on the development of new ways to design and execute rides and displays; and create attractions that could be brought back to Disneyland. Negotiations began with several corporations and in the end agreements were made with the Ford Motor Company, General Electric, and Pepsi-Cola; the state of Illinois also commissioned an attraction. Walt and his crew designed the Magic Skyway for Ford, which their 1963 corporate annual report described as "a memorable trip in Company-built convertibles through an entertaining and educational fantasy created by Walt Disney." Walt called it "a drama of prehistoric days" because it used animatronic dinosaurs in the one part that got transported back to Disneyland when the fair was over (it can still be seen during the train ride).

One of the most spectacular developments to come out of the New York World's Fair was this advancement in the quality and scope of Audio-Animatronics, the technology by which animation was given to three-dimensional figures and animals. It was taking the concepts of cartoon animations and giving them to real objects; it was another creation of the "illusion of life," and it advanced the field of robotics and machine simulation. In one of his television programs, Walt explained that they had been preparing for the developments they introduced at the World's Fair for years "without realizing it." Walt pointed to the work on the giant squid of *20,000 Leagues under the Sea* (1954) and the work before the opening of Disneyland with the developments in this "new field of animation."[14]

Walt had incorporated earlier versions of three-dimensional illusions of life in his work. When he was working on his miniature dioramas he had some of his engineers develop a display sometimes called the Dancing Man with actor Buddy Ebsen as a model (Ebsen was as famous for his dancing as for being Davy Crockett's sidekick). The Dancing Man was small but he attempted to recreate actual vaudeville dance steps; it was an experiment in imitating real human motion. When Disneyland opened, the mechanical animals in the "Jungle Cruise" highlighted the limitation of natural movement with the available technology. When the "Rainbow Cavern Mine Train" was changed into the "Mine Train through Nature's Wonderland" in 1960, animated animals were added throughout. The opening of the "Enchanted Tiki Room" at Disneyland in 1963 demonstrated the advancements Walt's team had made. The birds (as well as masks and flowers) talked and sang and while the movements weren't "natural" they were coordinated to the soundtrack and like a cartoon provided the wonderful illusion of stepping into an entirely possible fantastic world.

The search for a way to create believable mechanical life goes back much further than Walt's tinkering with the Dancing Man or the mechanical toys he purchased on his trips and later took apart to see their workings. Ancient mythologies, fairy tales, and folklore have stories of statues or machines that come to life including Pygmalion and Coppélia. Automatons, mechanical beings who performed actions like playing music, drawing, writing, and dancing, were a fascination in the 18th century. The early filmmaker Georges Méliès had a collection of such machines.[15] Artificial life was seen as a goal of all sorts of fields, including medicine, robotics, genetics, biology, chemistry, and philosophy.

Besides the dinosaurs and prehistoric humans that occupied the Ford exhibit, all three of the other World's Fair projects incorporated Audio-Animatronics with varying degrees of sophistication. The "it's a small world" display in the Pepsi-Cola pavilion, designed to celebrate UNICEF (United Nations International Children's Emergency Fund), featured hundreds of animated dolls singing the infectious song "It's a Small World." It still occupies a place at Disneyland and has been replicated at other versions of the park. Walt also had his staff design the Tower of the Four Winds, a kinetic sculpture that was in front of the Pepsi pavilion, but it was not saved after the fair. The attraction for General Electric was named "Progressland," and it has been called Walt's favorite. It featured an Audio-Animatronics family going through several stages of the 20th century and their interactions with electrical technology. It too featured a catchy tune, "There's a Great Big Beautiful Tomorrow." It came back to Disneyland after the World's Fair as the "Carousel of Progress" but now resides in Florida.

The most advanced Audio-Animatronics were applied to the exhibit for the State of Illinois. "Great Moments with Mr. Lincoln" became a spectacular hit (as did all the other Disney displays), and it demonstrated a technology that convincingly replicated human movement. The technology was not refined before Walt committed to do the Lincoln exhibit, and it was hours of extra work to get everything working. The exhibit featured a life-size Abraham Lincoln figure. The first head of Lincoln took a year to perfect and the entire body had to be programmed for dozens of different movements. In the performance, Lincoln, generated by electronics and hydraulics, rose and gave a speech that included parts of the Gettysburg Address (remember that Walt had once dressed as Lincoln and gave that speech to his classmates). The production of the Lincoln figure was filled with trials and errors all the way to opening day and beyond. The enormous problems supposedly led one designer to quip, "Do you suppose God is mad at Walt for creating Man in his own image?"[16] A duplicate of the Lincoln figure was created and placed in a show at Disneyland in 1966; parts of the original were found years later and displayed in a 50th anniversary museum show. A ticket for the show explained that it was there "so young people may have a better knowledge of the man who played such an important part in American History."[17]

The World's Fair work provided new exhibits for Disneyland, an enhanced reputation for WED and its production capabilities, and proof to Walt that the East Coast was open to his type of entertainment. But Walt had more than entertainment in mind. He had always been interested in concepts of the future, what the world would be like with different forms of transportation, education, housing, work, environment, technology, and amusements. His first work at Tomorrowland focused some of these ideas and through the years he worked with scientists and other futurists to present these ideas in his television series. Walt consulted with Wernher von Braun, the German rocket scientist, who worked with him on three television programs about space exploration.

Walt had his company buy up thousands of acres of land in Florida, close to where his parents had once lived for a few years. When Walt looked at the East Coast Disneyland, it was not just a new amusement park. The Florida Project, as it was first called, was attached to a larger set of ideas. It would include a permanent World's Fair and an international land that would celebrate the architecture and customs of the world—and as a result promote further understanding between cultures. The futurist concept that Walt was most interested in was called EPCOT, Experimental Prototype Community of Tomorrow, a model community of 20,000 people. It would also be a way to test out the urban planning and utopian ideas that fascinated Walt. It would be a showcase for solutions to urban problems. It would make people happy.

As Walt described it, "I don't believe there is a challenge anywhere in the world that is more important to people everywhere than finding the solution to the problems of our cities. But where do we begin? Well, we're convinced we must start with the public need. And the need is not just for curing the old ills of old cities. We think the need is for starting from scratch on virgin land and building a community that will become a prototype for the future."[18]

Planned or intentional communities were nothing new. After World War II, several Levittown communities (in New York and Pennsylvania) were planned and built whole, thought out as suburban areas with shared spaces, shopping, schools, and traffic controls but also rules designed to make behavior more uniform and inoffensive. Milton Hershey, of chocolate fame, planned and built a community for his workers around his factory in Pennsylvania. It was designed as an ideal place away from urban blight, and besides affordable quality housing, it had a community center, gardens, zoo, theatres, and a museum. He also built Hershey Park in 1907 as an amusement center for entertainment. The park still operates today. Most planned communities are privately controlled, and the applicability of their design to other situations is still questioned today. At more than 27,000 acres, Disney World had the luxury of shutting out the outside world even more.

Walt Disney World achieved the goals of a planned community not with its unsuccessful town, "Celebration, Florida" in the 1990s but by offering visitors the basic things that were lacking in most urban and rural settings. Like Disneyland, the place was safe and there was no fear of the other people walking about; most everyone was exhibiting self-control. There was civility, even friendliness, from both the staff and other visitors. There were no polluting or dangerous vehicles; walking was encouraged; and there was transportation for the disabled. It was green with trees and flowers; it was clean and pretty; it had convenient shopping and restaurants; it made sense.[19] It was how life was supposed to be.

But it was not the community Walt planned because it was still a vacation destination, not an everyday experience. Nevertheless, each year it was visited by more people than any other similar facility in the world. Ray Bradbury commented, "Thousands of city planners, urban redevelopers, ramshackle architects, big-time builders will march through Walt Disney World in the next 20 years, and go home wondering: 'Where can I buy a bottle of that stuff marked "Drink Me" so I can get drunk on Walt's dream, rebuild my town, replant the city gardens, reinvigorate the fountains, collect sun power, rethink the citizens, replan our future, bigger if need be, smaller where necessary?'"[20]

Walt worked on Disney World in Florida until he died in December 1966. After his death, his brother Roy continued the work until Walt Disney World was dedicated in 1971. Roy died soon after that.

As Walt's life was coming to an end, his contributions to American life continued to be recognized and awarded. Walt received the Presidential Medal of Freedom from President Johnson in 1964. It is considered one of the highest civilian awards in the country, given for "an especially meritorious contribution to the security or national interests of the United States, or to world peace, or to cultural or other significant public or private endeavors." Also being awarded the same day as Walt were humanitarian Helen Keller, poet Carl Sandburg, and writer John Steinbeck. About them President Johnson said, "Collectively, they have made man's world safe, his physical body more durable, his mind broader, his leisure more delightful, his standard of living higher and his dignity important. They are creators; we are the beneficiaries." The citation for Walt's medal summed up his life's work and read "Artist and impresario, in the course of entertaining an age, Walt Disney has created an American folklore."

Ray Bradbury summed up the reason we needed a Walt Disney. It is the same reason that we need to be engaged with both reality and fantasy. He once stated, "You have to dream yourself into being. The purpose of fiction is not to nail you to the ground as facts do, but to take you to the edge of the cliff and kick you off so you build your wings on the way down."[21] For Walt Disney's fellow genius and friend, Ray Bradbury, and for millions of people all over the world, Walt Disney was the guy who gave us that kick.

NOTES

1. Barstow, Robbins. *Disneyland Dream: The Fantastic, Real-Life, Dream-Come-True Adventure of the Barstow Family of Wethersfield, Connecticut.* 1956. Available at *Internet Archive,* http://www.archive.org/details/barstow_disneyland_dream_1956. Accessed April 11, 2010.

2. Williams, Pat, and James Denney. *How to Be Like Walt.* Deerfield Beach, Fla.: Health Communications, 2004, pp. 184–85.

3. Haveley, Julian. "Disneyland and Las Vegas." *Nation,* June 17, 1958, p. 511.

4. Bradbury, Ray. "Letter to the Editor." *Nation,* June 28, 1958.

5. *Disneyland USA: Special Historical Broadcasts*. 2001. DVD.

6. Green, Amy Boothe, and Howard E. Green. *Remembering Walt: Favorite Memories of Walt Disney*. New York: Hyperion, 1999, p. 167.

7. Hopper, Hedda. "Disneyland Preview Reveals Wonderland." *Los Angeles Times*, July 16, 1955, p. 14.

8. Hulse, Jerry. "Dream Realized—Disneyland Opens." *Los Angeles Times*, July 18, 1955; p. A1.

9. Hill, Gladwin. "A World Walt Disney Created." *New York Times*, July 31, 1955, p. X17.

10. "Disneyland Opens Gates to Thousands." *Los Angeles Times*, July 19, 1955, p. 2.

11. Weiss, Werner. *Yesterland*, "Disneyland One Year Old." Available at http://www.yesterland.com/oneyear.html. Accessed April 11, 2010.

12. Miller, Diane Disney, and Pete Martin. "Small Boy's Dream Comes True." *Saturday Evening Post*, January 5, 1957, p. 81.

13. Mason, Katie. "Disneyland: From Dream to Reality." *Animation World Magazine*, December 1998.

14. "Disneyland Goes to the World's Fair." *Walt Disney's Wonderful World of Color*, May 17, 1964.

15. Wood, Gaby. *Living Dolls: A Magical History of the Quest for Mechanical Life*. London: Faber and Faber Limited, 2002, p. 181.

16. Green and Green, p. 171.

17. See the ticket at http://vintageisneylandtickets.blogspot.com/2009/04/great-moments-with-mr-lincoln-first.html. Accessed April 11, 2010.

18. "It All Began With a Man: A Biography Of Walt Disney." *Walt Disney Archives*. Available at http://d23.disney.go.com/library/000000_WDA_AL_WaltDisneyBio.html. Accessed April 11, 2010.

19. Fjellman, Stephen M. *Vinyl Leaves: Walt Disney World and America*. Boulder, Colo.: Westview Press, 1992, pp. 200–203.

20. Sampson, Wade. "Ray Bradbury Shares Walt Disney's Vision and Legacy. MousePlanet, February 27, 2008. Available at http://www.mouseplanet.com/8237/Ray_Bradbury_Shares_Walt_Disneys_Vision_and_Legacy. Accessed April 11, 2010.

21. O'Leary, Devin. "Grandfather Time: An Interview with Ray Bradbury." *Weekly Alibi*, September 27, 1999. Available at http://www.weeklywire.com/ww/09-27-99/alibi_feat1.html. Accessed April 11, 2010.

APPENDIX: THE WALT DISNEY OF . . .

Not everyone likes Walt Disney. Not everyone agrees that Disneyland is the Happiest Place on Earth. But it is hard to deny that Walt has had an immense influence on American culture. His influence is so wide-spread and far reaching that we have several words for this spread of all things Disney: Disneyization, Disnification, Disnified, Disneyesque, Disneyed, Disneyfication, Distorifying history or making it "Distory" (Disney's history). These terms are all negative evaluations, complaints about the process of removing the genuine and authentic from our cultural practices and replacing it with the ubiquitous, banal, sanitized, colonizing, homogenized, soulless, inauthentic, profitable, consumerist, unnatural, plasticized, or synthetic things and practices that they associate with Disney, either the corporation or the man. For this approach, Walt is a cultural problem, an example of what can go wrong when one man, or one vision of the world, comes to dominate our approach to everyday life.

On the other hand, there are those who still look to Walt Disney for a model of behavior. Soon after Walt's death, a concept of Walt's "traditions" was developed, guidelines for how to be like Walt, how to understand his philosophy and think like him. Ideas that guided his life—being nice to everyone, believing that people are good, working on things you love—have been formalized into workshops, books, and corporate training sessions.

In addition, people everywhere also apply these concepts—both the good and the bad—to their everyday lives without any special training. Walt Disney has become a metaphor for things that are high quality, creative, and the best of their class as well as those that are commercial, crass, and designed to make money. The various uses of "Walt Disney" or the Disney name in general shows how people use analogies to Disney to draw attention to the special qualities they share.

The Disney Of:

- Japanese director Hayao Miyazaki, who directed *Princess Mononoke* in 1997, is considered the "Disney of Japan" because he has made what are considered the best and most popular animations in that country.[1]
- Animator Osamu Tezuka is also the "Walt Disney of Japan."[2]
- Hergé (creator of the comic TinTin) is the "Disney of Belgium" because he revolutionized comic book and cartoon art in Europe the same way Walt Disney did in America.[3]
- The World Wrestling Federation (WWF) used to be considered the "Disney of wrestling" until they changed to more violent shows because of the television competition of other wrestling organizations.[4]
- "Is it just us, or is Ferrari slowly taking its place as the Disney of the automotive world?" asks an automobile blog.[5]
- Skagway, an Alaskan town from the gold rush days that now plays host to cruise ships, is the "Disney of the North" and its town is "Disneyesque" because it "looked too perfect and cute to be real."[6]
- Singapore is "Disneyland with the death penalty," wrote acclaimed author of science fiction, William Gibson, in *Wired* magazine in 1993. To Gibson, they both are conformist and lacking in creativity, and feel like a large corporation runs them.[7]

- Prodigy, an Internet information and Web access service of the 1990s, was the "Disney of on-line companies" because it made a stance to provide a family oriented service and did not allow the posting of materials that it considered inappropriate.[8]
- Jiri Trnka is the Walt Disney of the East because the puppet animation of this Czechoslovakian artist was so detailed and innovative.[9]
- Bill Gates may turn out to be the Walt Disney of the Web.[10]
- Shigeru Miyamoto, the creator of early video game Donkey Kong and the Nintendo character, Mario, is the "Walt Disney of our time" because he has "unleashed mass entertainment with a global breadth, cultural endurance and financial success unsurpassed since Disney's fabled career." Miyamoto oversees Nintendo game designs and is credited with developing the Wii gaming platform.[11]
- Ikea is the "Disney of interior design," and this is evident when visiting their stores, which resemble theme parks with rides, restaurants, and parking attendants.[12]
- 37 signals, a Web software company that develops online applications, is called the "Disney of software" on the company's promotional Web site. But some readers disagree with the pretentious headline, pointing out that Disney (or Apple and Lotus, which it is also compared to) has "world-class, trendsetting, and beautiful design—and the prices to match" while this company does the opposite.[13]
- Cirque du Soleil is becoming the "Disney of the New Age" because like the Disney corporation it has "morphed from a happy-go-lucky creative commune into a streamlined, hard-nosed, far-sighted and profit-wise conglomerate."[14]
- A theme park in Buenos Aires, Argentina, named Tierra Santa is the "Disney of religion" because it "offers a religious experience drenched in kitsch."[15]
- Holt Renfrew & Co. Ltd. (a Canadian department store chain) is the "Disney of the fashion world" for its seemingly magical work environment that attracts employees with substantial discounts and other benefits.[16]

- SONY is called the "Disney of consumer electronics" because it has dominated that market.[17]
- Steve Axtell is the "Walt Disney of puppet makers" for creating innovative character puppets that are remote control. He is compared to Walt, who provided the model of a creative person who honed his skills, stuck to a vision, and then expanded his initial activities by innovating and using the latest technologies.[18]
- According to one blog (RepChatter) that considers reputation as the measure of all things, McDonald's has become the "Disney of fast food." Their interest in associating one of America's most common sources of food with Disney is somewhat indirect: "TV commercials highlighting artery-clogging fries and burgers are just as important to Mickey D's ongoing success as Pinocchio, The Lion King and The Little Mermaid are to Disney." The general concern seems to be the influence on the lives of unsuspecting children.[19]
- In a review of its new iPad, Apple is likened to "the Disney of technology, always adding a dash of 'magic' to its products."[20]
- The "Disney of basketmakers" is a company called Longaberger, which makes handcrafted baskets.[21]
- A shopping mall in Dubai (Madinat Jumeirah) is called the Arab consumerism theme park—as lifeless and dull as all of the other malls. It's the Disney of shopping in Dubai.[22]
- The "Disney of Irish bars" is the Briny Irish pub in Fort Lauderdale, Florida.[23]
- The Dafen Musical Theatre in Taiwan is "widely regarded as the Disney of the East" because their presentations are "ideal family entertainment."[24]
- The Dalian Discovery Land theme park in northern China is considered the "Disney" of China.[25]
- A company called Visualization Navigator, Ltd., is proud to announce that they have been called "the Disney of data" in the environmental world. This means they are creative and innovative in their field.[26]
- Because Wegmans, a grocery-store chain, "epitomizes the forward thinking and creative methods used to generate and keep business," it is called the "Disney" of the retail food industry.[27]

- Gunther von Hagens, who has made popular exhibits plasticizing real human bodies, has been called the "Disney of Death."[28]
- Machu Picchu, an ancient ruin in Peru, is the "Disney of the Andes" because 2,000 people visit it every day.[29]
- The "Disney of the wine tasting world" is the Spier Wine farm located in Capetown, South Africa, because it has busloads of tourists and large group wine tastings.[30]
- The Hofbrauhaus in Munich, Germany, is the "Disney" of beer halls because "rather than a homely and cozy feel" of a local beer hall, one travel blog explains, "the Hofbrauhaus was overflowing with tourists sitting and large benches singing loudly, clinking glasses and swilling 1L steins of beer."[31]
- The Roland Martin Marina in Florida is the "Disney of fishing."[32]

NOTES

Note: All accessed July 16, 2009.

1. http://lavender.fortunecity.com/attenborough/487/index.html
2. http://www.kimbawlion.com/rant2.htm
3. http://www.boston.com/travel/blog/2009/02/pen_in_hand.html
4. http://www.welovesoaps.net/2009/05/flashback-pro-wrestling-soap-opera-gone.html
5. http://www.autoblog.com/2006/11/24/at-maranello-village-the-prancing-horse-follows-you-home/
6. http://www.epinions.com/content_253448523396
7. http://www.wired.com/wired/archive/1.04/gibson.html
8. http://www.nytimes.com/1990/12/16/business/forum-the-1st-amendment-is-safe-at-prodigy.html
9. http://www.awn.com/mag/issue5.04/5.04pages/dutkatrnka.php3
10. http://www.businessweek.com/1996/43/b3498163.htm
11. http://games.slashdot.org/story/08/05/25/1759248/Shigeru-Miyamoto-The-Walt-Disney-of-Our-Time?art_pos=11
12. http://jasongraphix.com/journal/disney-of-interior-design/
13. http://www.37signals.com/svn/posts/1427–37signals-is-the-lotus-iphone-disney-of-software
14. http://www.thecanadianencyclopedia.com/index.cfm?PgNm=TCE&Params=M1ARTM0012886

15. http://www.canada.com/topics/travel/story.html?id=109835c5-458a-474c-8286-f0f9f687ba26

16. http://www.thestar.com/SpecialSections/Top50/article/170123

17. http://www.wired.com/wired/archive/11.09/start.html?pg=2

18. http://themoderatevoice.com/20624/steve-axtell-the-walt-disney-of-puppet-makers-unveils-hands-free-remote-controlled-puppets/

19. http://www.repmanblog.com/repman/2007/08/mcdonalds-has-b.html

20. http://features.techworld.com/security/3219000/identifying-apple-ipad-security-weaknesses/?olo=rss

21. http://divorce360webbeat.blogspot.com/search?q=disney

22. http://wikimapia.org/86318/Madinat-Jumeirah

23. http://moodvane.com/index.php?s=disney

24. http://www.taipeitimes.com/News/feat/archives/2006/07/14/2003318824

25. http://www.cntour365.com:8080/cntour365/Eng/dijie-dalian.jsp

26. http://www.visualizationavigator.com/

27. http://www.presentation-pointers.com/showarticle/articleid/530/

28. http://www.sciencemag.org/cgi/content/summary/301/5637/1172?tdate=%2F%2F&HITS=10&hits=10&fdate=%2F%2F&author1=Bohannon&maxtoshow=&FIRSTINDEX=0&resourcetype=HWCIT&titleabstract=Ginther+von+Hagens&searchid=1&RESULTFORMAT=

29. http://www.sarahandjeff.org/node/8

30. http://www.accessiblecapetown.com/winelands.html

31. http://www.travelblog.org/Europe/Germany/Bavaria/Munich/blog-365097.html

32. http://www.frommers.com/destinations/treasurecoast/0390010011.html

FURTHER READING

The following books are recommended for further reading on Walt Disney's life. Not all agree with the approach taken in this book, but each provides a different emphasis that both complicates and clarifies Walt Disney's intricate life:

Barrier, Michael. *The Animated Man: A Life of Walt Disney*. Berkeley: University of California Press, 2007.

Finch, Christopher. *The Art of Walt Disney: From Mickey Mouse to the Magic Kingdoms*. Rev. and expanded ed. New York: H. N. Abrams, 2004.

Gabler, Neal. *Walt Disney: The Triumph of the American Imagination*. New York: Knopf, 2006.

Thomas, Bob. *Walt Disney: An American Original*. New York: Hyperion, 1994.

Thomas, Frank, and Ollie Johnston. *The Illusion of Life: Disney Animation*. New York: Hyperion, 1995.

Watts, Steven. *The Magic Kingdom: Walt Disney and the American Way of Life*. Boston: Houghton Mifflin, 1997.

In recent years, much of the valuable information on Walt Disney has been available on various fan Web sites and blogs. The following are recommended for the access they provide to documents and original insights:

Carolwood Foundation and Society at http://www.carolwood.com/
Disney History at http://disneybooks.blogspot.com/
D23 at http://d23.disney.go.com/library/000000_WDA_AL_WaltDisneyBio.html
INDUCKS at http://inducks.org/
Just Disney at http://www.justdisney.com/
Laughing Place at http://www.laughingplace.com/default.asp
Michael Barrier at http://www.michaelbarrier.com/
Mickey News at http://www.MickeyNews.com/
Mouse Planet at http://www.mouseplanet.com/
Stuff from the Park at http://matterhorn1959.blogspot.com/
Vintage Disneyland Goodies at http://vintagedisneylandgoodies.blogspot.com/
Wade's Wayback Machine by Wade Sampson at http://www.mouseplanet.com/search.php?type=w&aid=ws
Walt Disney Family Museum at http://disney.go.com/disneyatoz/familymuseum/index.html
Yesterland at http://www.yesterland.com/yester.html

INDEX

About the Author

Dr. LOUISE KRASNIEWICZ is an anthropologist and media producer whose research focuses on mainstream American movies, fan culture, narrative, and rituals. She teaches courses on movies as a form of mythology and as stories about other possible worlds, like those worlds studied by anthropologists. She is a Lecturer in the Department of Anthropology and a Consulting Scholar in the Cultural Heritage Center at the University of Pennsylvania. She is coauthor with Michael Blitz of two other biographies in this series: *Johnny Depp* and *Arnold Schwarzenegger*. She is also coauthor with Blitz of the study of Arnold Schwarzenegger's rise to power, *Why Arnold Matters: The Rise of a Cultural Icon* (Basic Books, 2004). She currently resides in Bryn Mawr, Pennsylvania.